D1594701

Exploring Earthiness

Exploring

EARTHINESS

The Reality and Perception
of Being Human Today

Anne Primavesi

CASCADE *Books* · Eugene, Oregon

EXPLORING EARTHINESS
The Reality and Perception of Being Human Today

Cascade Books
An Imprint of Wipf and Stock Publishers
199 W. 8th Ave., Suite 3
Eugene, OR 97401

www.wipfandstock.com

ISBN 13: 978-1-62032-468-4

Cataloging-in-Publication data:

Primavesi, Anne.

 Exploring earthiness : the reality and perception of being human today / Anne Primavesi.

 xxii + 154 p.; 23 cm—Includes bibliographical references and index.

 ISBN 13: 978-1-62032-468-4

 1. Nature—Religious aspects. 2. Gaia hypothesis. 3. Human ecology—Religious aspects. I. Title.

BT695.5 .P77 2013

Manufactured in the USA.

For James Lovelock,
whose scientific vision of Gaia-Earth
gave us a new vision of ourselves.

The Gift of Gaian Identity

unknown to the family
whose name I claim as mine
being grown
before familiar time
breaking through
and beyond
recognized bounds
of ages, race, place, kind, creed
to kin
taking a liminal pace
forward from sea onto shores
now lifted into familiar skylines
within which we trace a descent
transcending known identities
gifted into becoming known
as a Gaian being

Table of Contents

Acknowledgments

It is clear from the foreword of this book that it has been inspired by the dedication, insights, and hard work of the many people I have met and worked with before and after the United Nations Conference on Environment and Development in Rio in 1992. Since then, particular inspiration and support has come from the Gaianet Group at the Royal Geological Society, London, and in Ireland from our friend Lucy Mooney, and the many religious groups dedicated to living and sharing an ecologically friendly lifestyle.

The book itself could not have been written without the wide-ranging written sources made accessible by the Celia and Edward James Library Fund. Mary Midgley's encouragement kept me going while her incisive comments ensured my arguments and conclusions had their necessary force. Above all, Mark Primavesi's loving support and close reading of the whole text is integral to it. And the arduous task of getting it ready for publication has also been his.

Foreword

This book is a gift to all of us who are concerned about global warming, climate change, poisonous living environments, and the growing disparity between the 1 percent and the 99 percent. Completed when Hurricane Sandy had wreaked havoc on the Northeast seaboard of the United States, this book is a timely wake-up call to all of us.

With clarity and rigor, Anne Primavesi traces the root causes of human beings' alienation from the earth and offers a new image of Earthiness as Oneness, defining it as "a material, shared global state of being alive; with all life being supported by planetary resources held in common."

Primavesi takes us on a journey through the desacralization of the land, the disdain of the earth, and the adoption of a utilitarian attitude toward nature and its resources in the West. She analyzes the dualism in the philosophical ideas of Plato and Descartes, the statements about property and ownership in Locke's works on government, and the ascendancy of technical rationality since the Enlightenment. She challenges the domination of mind over body, human beings over nature, and reason over all other faculties. The result of this domination is a downward spiral in which the resourceful earth has become something to be exploited, colonized, and conquered for profits and human greed.

The global Occupy Movement in 2011 has shown that there is a limit to runaway capitalism and corporate greed. Protesters in North Africa, the Middle East, Europe, North America, and in other parts of the world have stood up to demand the end of corrupted government, the bailouts of large banks, the concentration of wealth, and dysfunctional economic and political systems. More than ever, there is a collective awareness that the ways we have conducted our lives are not sustainable. Occupy Wall Street declared: "2011 will be remembered as a year of revolution, the beginning of the end for an unsustainable global system based on poverty, oppression, and violence."

Primavesi points out that fundamental institutional changes will not come about until we have changed our habits of thinking. Any changes will only be skin deep unless we complete the Copernican revolution of not giving superiority to human beings by placing them at the center of the universe. This requires us to recover the ancient wisdom found in many traditions: that we are earthly beings—part of Earthiness.

She concludes the book with an elaboration of the gift of Gaian identity, based on James Lovelock's Gaia theory. Instead of tracing our identity through familial, national, and political, or religious genealogies, Lovelock asks us to broaden our awareness and to ground it firmly within the evolutionary lineages of the whole Earth community. We are inescapably related to all things. With such a wholistic and planetary perspective, we can renew our covenant to each other and to the earth and embark on a new journey.

As a Chinese theologian, I find that Primavesi's ideas resonate with many of those I have inherited from Chinese philosophy and poetry. The neo-Confucian scholar Zhang Zai (1020–1077 CE) had a famous saying that echoes the themes she presents in this book:

> Heaven is my father and earth is my mother, and even such a small being as I finds an intimate place in their midst. Therefore, that which fills the universe I regard as my body and that which directs the universe I regard as my nature. All people are my brothers and sisters, and all things are my companions.

Classical Chinese poetry is full of images of nature. The Chinese sense of beauty and harmony, influenced by Daoism and Buddhism, is defined so much by nature and the agricultural cycles.

As I have worked on the themes of postcolonialism and theology, this book provides me with much food for thought. I value Primavesi's challenge to Constantinian Christianity, with its divine right of kings, and the social and ecclesiastical hierarchies human beings have created. What she asks for is nothing less than fresh and revolutionary thinking about Christianity and with that, the reversal of many commonly accepted concepts about God, the church, and human beings that we are culturally accustomed to, whether or not we are Christians.

I once invited Primavesi to speak to my class. She challenged the students to see that hierarchical systems—when viewed as a triangular form in which power is concentrated at the top—can be found in all areas of our lives. Its power dynamics remain the status quo unless we are committed to changing it and offering alternatives to it. She tore up a piece of paper to make a

Möbius strip and used it as an image that shows we are one, continuous, and interrelated.

Twenty years ago, Primavesi and I attended the conference organized by the World Council Churches during the 1992 United Nations Conference on Environment and Development meeting in Rio de Janeiro. During the conference, many ecologically conscious theologians, from North and South, spoke and articulated the visions of a new heaven and a new earth. We were grateful to the non-governmental organizations for producing *The Earth Charter*, much of which continues to be valid today. In commemorating the twentieth anniversary of the Rio meeting and the *Charter*, I am glad that Primavesi offers her new insights by starting with the *Charter*'s opening words: "We are the Earth." We need these insights now more than ever.

Kwok Pui-lan

Preface

> Blessed be you, mighty matter, irresistible march of evolution, re-
> ality ever new-born; you who, by constantly shattering our mental
> categories, force us to go ever further and further in our pursuit
> of the truth.[1]

Twenty years ago I came back from the 1992 United Nations Conference on
Environment and Development in Rio with a very important document: *The
Earth Charter*. It was produced, after much debate, by the Non-Governmental
Organizations (NGOs) gathered there. When, after my return, I was asked to
speak about the Conference to a group in Britain, I began with the Preamble
to the Charter. Its opening sentence runs:

> We are Earth: the people, plants and animals, rains and oceans,
> breath of the forest and flow of the sea.[2]

As I read and commented on this, squirming, shuffling and subdued mutter-
ing gradually increased and eventually emerged into protests such as:
    *"We're not Earth! We are more than Earth! Other than Earth! Different
from Earth!"*
    Some went further, stressing what appears to make us different from all
other Earth creatures:
    *"Our bodies came from Earth; but we have souls and minds and intellects
that make us distinct from, superior to, in charge of all other earthly creatures."*
This was a defining moment for me. It revealed both predominant attitudes
to our "earthiness" and the strength of what Teilhard de Chardin calls "our
mental categories." It also revealed the need to "shatter" them. The difficulty
of doing so, however, became all too clear as the meeting progressed and has
become even clearer since then. A major reason for this was (and is) a long

---

1. De Chardin, *Hymn of the Universe*, 68.
2. See *The Earth Charter* (UNCED 1992) in Appendix 1.

established Western religious, intellectual and cultural education system that unquestioningly assumes the superiority of the human species, albeit on a variety of grounds. They include our sole possession of the faculty of reason; or of an immortal soul; or of a divine mandate to govern and use the Earth, its resources and other species for our own purposes.

> Descartes's famous definition of existence (I think, therefore I am) completes a new myth about our relationship to the world; human beings are the things that think (the only things, and that is all they are) and the rest of the world is made up of things that can be measured (or "thought about"). Subject or object, mind or body, matter or spirit: this is the dual world we have inherited—where the brain's ability to distinguish and classify has ruled the roost. From this duality come the ideas we live by, what William Blake called "mind-forged manacles," the mental abstractions that seem too obvious to question, that construct and confine our vision of reality.[3]

Mary Midgley notes an important reason for the enduring appeal of this dualistic view of ourselves. It lies in an acceptance that conflict is a reality in human life and the desire to explain it. Whereas Darwin locates conflict *within human nature itself*, that is, between our various naturally incompatible motives, western Christianity has followed Paul's position in his Epistle to the Galatians:

> The flesh lusteth against the spirit and the spirit against the flesh and these are contrary to one another, so that you cannot do the things that you would (Gal 5:17–23).

This kind of entanglement between the moral life and mind-body dualism, which the Christian tradition drew from Plato, has repeatedly involved it in a dualist drama that has led to a great deal of unnecessary contempt and fear, both of the body itself and of the affections seen as belonging to it. It has also been used, Midgley says, to justify brutality to non-human animals on the grounds that they are not supposed to have souls. It persists in a special reverence for human intelligence, seen as almost supernatural, and even in an exaltation of virtual experiences over those that involve (earthly) flesh.[4]

This solitary self-image has scarcely changed over time, despite scientific endorsements and seeming cultural acceptance of evolutionary views of human life. A major obstacle is the fact that social mechanisms that link our contemporary experience to that of previous generations generally lack any

3. Suzuki and McConnell, *The Sacred Balance*, 192.
4. Midgley, *The Solitary Self*, 97–99.

organic and continuous relation to our earthly history. The effects of this cultural apartheid and divided worldview place each of us as a mind inside the limits of our bodies. This, we believe, is the edge of *me*, this layer of skin; this is the organism I propel through the world, surrounded by things, receiving sensory messages—smells, tastes, sights—through various orifices and nerve endings, which may help me to know the world outside; or may turn out to be dangerous misconceptions:

> This idea of the body as a machine—quite new in the history of our species—has produced technology to remedy its limits; more machines to extend the reach, accelerate the motion, and magnify the strength and sensory acuity of this body machine as it acts on the world beyond. Mind within body—the ghost within the machine—that is what our culture teaches us we are, what we accept as obvious and normal and real.[5]

A major factor in this cultural disengagement from and disharmony with the land emerged in Rio: the growth of mega-cities in which billions of people are born, live, and die without any direct sensory experience of our relationship to and dependence on Earth's resources. In capitalist cultures, these visible obstacles to recognizing such dependence are religiously supported by the Christian belief that Earth exists solely "for man's use and benefit"; with that "benefit" now understood almost solely in terms of monetary gain. The destructive conduct endorsed by this presumption has increased in proportion to the growth of every country's GDP; with an accompanying shift in the perception of "wealth" from earthly abundance to "money." Or, in contemporary terms, from shared planetary resources to "shares" on the Stock Exchange; from our common future to commodity "futures."

Throughout the following chapters the economic origins and course of this shift in European cultures will be explored. The stress, however, will be on the decisive cultural and religious effects of the Emperor Constantine's conversion in 312 CE and the consequent "Romanization" of Christianity. Two main reasons for this approach that appear unrelated to each other can with hindsight be seen as interdependent. The first is the militarist character of that Empire, both before and after its Christianization, with its ever-increasing appropriation of land and ruthless subjugation of peoples through war and slavery. The territorial reach and effects of this on human populations have been extensively recorded. But their religious, economic, and environmental effects went far wider and deeper. Briefly here, the cult of the Roman gods and of the Emperor as divine, as *Dei Filius*, gave a religious legitimacy to war and

---

5. Suzuki and McConnell, *The Sacred Balance*, 192–93.

acquisition of territory that would be invoked time and again in later centuries and recorded in the advance of Christian colonization worldwide from the fifteenth century onwards.

The second factor is a desacralization of Earth, or Gaia, that legitimized appropriation and exploitation of the lands of conquered peoples. Both these factors are graphically presented in the pre-Christian Great Altar of Pergamon, a faithful ally of Rome in the eastern Mediterranean. It was erected by Eumenes II between 180–160 BCE to commemorate the conquest of the Galatians, depicting this as "the triumph of civilization over primeval chaos." In her detailed description and interpretation of the Roman semiotics of the frieze, Brigitte Kahl concentrates attention on the human figures involved, notably that of "The Dying Trumpeter." My interest centers, however, on the East Frieze with its archetypal mythic depiction of "Victory and Defeat." There, next to Zeus, his daughter Athena wrestles with Alkyoneus, the youngest and favorite son of Gaia, the Earth Goddess.

This scene, says Kahl, is the most pathetic of those in the Great Frieze, and the only one featuring a female opponent of the gods and goddesses above her.

> Reaching out from the ground which covers her body up to her breasts, Gaia raises her arms in a desperate plea for mercy. Her cornucopia, the horn-shaped vessel overflowing with a bounty of fruit, appears in her left hand. With her right hand she tries to hold on to her giant son Alkyoneus, who remained invulnerable as long as he could keep contact with the motherly ground. But Athena's elegantly draped leg intervenes from above between the two of them. . . . As he is about to lose the life-preserving connection, the deadly poison of Athena's snake penetrates his chest and his face is torn in pain and despair. Directly above, unmoved by the tragedy of Gaia and her son, the winged goddess, Nike, is approaching to adorn Athena with the crown of triumph.[6]

From the sixth century BCE onwards, says Kahl, this battle became a well-established iconographic theme and gradually came to define foreign peoples encountered in the process of colonization, whether as slaves or as prisoners resulting from war. It laid the foundation, she says, for some of the most fundamental polarizations that have shaped occidental identity constructs and western worldviews up to the present day.[7] My main concern is with the underlying battle with and "conquest" of Gaia-Earth and her fertile offspring. As Peter Brown shows, her "desacralization" into a resource base conquered

6. Kahl, *Galatians Re-Imagined*, 92–93.
7. Ibid., 94–96.

and ruled by divinely mandated human force played a crucial role in the later Romanization of Christianity.

Firstly, it brought about a crucial shift in attitudes to "wealth" in terms of both earthly and monetary resources. This entailed an understanding of the "transferability" of "wealth" from earth to heaven through humdrum acts of giving. Gifts to the poor and donations to the churches could build a real Christian "future": both here and in the afterlife. Hence such chapter headings as:

> Whatever somebody for the sake of his salvation and the repose of his soul will have donated . . . to the venerable church on behalf of the poor.[8]

In today's secular culture, attempts to reconstruct or describe this mindset have a decidedly ironic ring. For it required an imaginative religious exercise in what has been characterized as "salvation economics":

> Go part shares with God for your possessions and render to the Supreme Father thanks for the gift that has been given to you by Him. . . . You and your household can keep all that you possess, provided that you take good care to declare that God is the donor of these things as well.[9]

Secondly, this quote from Paulinus of Nola implies that the landowner did not owe his wealth to the abundance miraculously fostered by the little gods of the countryside. Rather, the providence of the One God reached down in a great arc through every level of Roman society to touch the fields and those who owned them. This followed a wider shift in Christian attitudes toward society and the imperial system in particular. To think that wealth lay in the hands of a single, all-powerful God, to whom they were accountable for its use, was a novel idea. The power and range of this change in attitude to the relationship between Earth and wealth cannot be underestimated. It effectively desacralized the land by cutting it down to size as human property: to be grasped ever tighter in the hands of landowners to value and exchange it for "money."

The trajectory of Christian colonization would spread this culture worldwide. While its religious justification has all but disappeared, its global effects are now all too evident. Originally, its sharply "vertical" view of the natural world (as existing for the landowner to accumulate money) was transposed to a higher plane where God was seen as the great *dominus*—the great landowner. And it was the *domini* themselves—the local landowners—who

---

8. Brown, *Through the Eye of a Needle*, 475.

9. Ibid., 237–38.

were "sharecroppers" of the Lord, holding their lands under God.[10] By the seventeenth century, as we shall see, John Locke's writings mark a tipping point between this religious model, its secular application in today's market culture and its material, global effects.

A major collective and personal effect has been an increasing ignorance of both the truth and significance of our own earthiness. Yet that truth is now being proven negatively—by the perceptible impact of human lifestyle and market transactions on Earth's climate and fruitfulness; and as a corollary, the now perceptible impact of climate change on ourselves. The latter is most notable in the lives of those most impoverished by these transactions. Together these call into question the common cultural understanding that Earth is our "property" to use and dispose of for monetary gain and in any way that increases it. Particularly over the past six centuries we have treated Earth and its inhabitants, human and more-than-human, as merchandise to be bought, sold, exploited, wasted, or discarded for money and status. The development, trajectory and effects of that attitude will be traced throughout the following chapters.

It now coincides, however, with a new and burgeoning scientific vision of the past, present and future of our universe; of the interactions between Earth's lifeforms and their environments and of our own relationship to the "irresistible march of evolution." Laurence Krauss, director of the Origins Project at Arizona State University, notes that we are like the early mapmakers redrawing the picture of the globe even as new continents were being discovered. Astrophysics has allowed us to glimpse the truth that in its earliest moments our universe and all its "mighty matter" were contained in a volume smaller than the size of an atom.

We also know that, since the Big Bang around 13.7 billion years ago, there are more than 100 billion galaxies in the observable universe. And that, as far as we know, Earth is unique within the Milky Way Galaxy within which it belongs. This uniqueness, centered in its ability to support life, drives home the disastrous nature of dominant religious, mental, and cultural categories that underlie the refusal to accept the fact of our earthiness. And continue to do so in spite of knowing that our being "human" means that we are made from *humus* (soil); and that every breath we take depends on the "world-mothering air" embracing our planet.[11]

The environments we have created for ourselves may have been and indeed are an extraordinary and unprecedented human achievement, constructed in large part by the awesome power of our abstracting, pattern-making

10. Ibid., 239.

11. Hopkins, *Poems*, 56.

brains. But their essential transience should evoke a Darwinian sense of awe at the fact that humanity is blessed simply by belonging within the irresistible march of the evolution of life on Earth. And that we belong there and nowhere else.

1

Resourceful Earth

One by one, pillars of classical logic have fallen by the wayside as science progressed in the 20th Century, from Einstein's realization that measurements of space and time were not absolute but observer-dependent, to quantum mechanics, which not only put fundamental limits to what we can empirically know but also showed that elementary particles and the atoms they form are doing a million seemingly impossible things at once.[1]

The pillars of classical logic may appear to have fallen into ruins like the Pergamon Frieze. But their mythic and religious strength continues to support a vertical, hierarchical view of our relationship with Earth, seemingly based on our own observations and presuppositions about ourselves. Our measurements of space and time have, it is true, expanded the limits of our knowledge. But this has not, as yet, shattered the human mental categories supporting a vertical vision of our being "in charge" of Earth: whether through divine appointment or by exercising our unique talents.

These latter have now brought us a realization that elementary particles and the atoms they form are not only the very "stuff" of Earth's body but also the "stuff" of our bodies also. And that just some of the seemingly impossible things they do at once are keeping us firmly balanced on Earth's surface while enabling us to take in the oxygen we need to breathe and the food (supplied

1. Krauss, *A Universe without Purpose.*

I

by Earth) that our bodies need to survive. Generally speaking, we take these relationships between Earth and ourselves for granted.

Also taken for granted by most of us nowadays are our evolutionary origins within the planetary community of life. Modern science and technologies enable us to see Earth as a whole; as one cosmic body that, over eons of time, has given life to a diversity of creatures that include ourselves. If asked, we would generally agree that these facts underpin the radical oneness and evolution of earthly life, including our own, from its beginnings to the present day. Our widespread use of the term "globalization" signals an increased appreciation that Earth's planetary systems have worked and continue to work as a whole in sustaining the lives of its multiplicity of beings.

Now, however, "globalization" also signals our failure to react positively to the implications of these scientific observations by reducing our demands on Earth's shared resource base. This is the dark side of human "globalizing": one that requires the reassessment of our own institutions and lifestyles, of their increasing pressure on shared resources and on Earth's ability to sustain life. Underpinning this dark side is a self-image of humans as "owners" and of these resources as our "property." This has led to a type of development worldwide in which what is really the common property of all species (the earthly commons) is being appropriated and gradually destroyed by us through the process of accumulating monetary wealth.

Peter Brown exposes the historic European origins of this process:

> Since the time of Hesiod and the great grain silos of the Bronze Age, the storage and sale of foodstuffs was an unchanging feature of the landscape of the Mediterranean. What changed significantly in the fourth century AD was the manner in which the tax system of the Roman Empire created a situation in which the rich were able to change food into gold to their great advantage. To sum up a complex development: from Constantine onward, the Roman state flooded the economy with gold. The gold solidus became the symbol of a new order.[2]

The later progress of this new order, known today as capitalism, will be followed up in some detail in later chapters. An important point made here by Brown is that by the end of the fourth century, a "poverty line" had come to be drawn in the social imagination of contemporary society: between the area of society where the mighty *solidus* circulated and a bleak social hinterland where the *solidus* was either absent or difficult to obtain. Translated into today's monetary terms, this is now the largely accepted and legally endorsed

---

2. Brown, *Through the Eye of a Needle*, 14f.

capitalist "life process" of civil and "civilized" societies worldwide. As such, it ignores the internal reality of our social relationships as well as our interactions with the "earthly" commons that, in scientific terms, constitute the planetary resource base below and above land and sea that sustains all earthly life.

The global abuse of those resources now demonstrates that capitalism takes no account of our total dependence on their durability and stability. At the same time, we are beginning to learn their parameters, which scientist Johan Rockström has defined in terms of planetary "boundaries." Within these (and nowhere else) we (and implicitly, all other creatures) can safely live and operate. They include climate change; ocean acidification; stratospheric ozone; biogeochemical nitrogen; phosphorus inflow to oceans; global freshwater use and the rate at which biological diversity is lost.[3] All of these contribute to and are essential for earthly life, including our own. Together, they are the common property of all life on Earth.

These boundaries that make life sustainable are set by the very nature of the Earth itself. However, they have been and are being broken through by us, most clearly by human population growth. This, together with our increasing consumption and consequent depletion of resources, has reached a level where not only our own future, but that of all life on Earth depends on a commitment from us to decrease our overuse of them. Rockström's scientific overview keeps many different projects in play; but the important point here is the fact that evolution by natural selection is a property of the whole planet, not just of its organisms alone: and certainly not of our species alone. This raises fundamental questions about the planetary nature and impact of our lives and lifestyles, questioning the motivations behind them and justifications for them.

These are questions that the natural sciences traditionally ignore. So scientific acceptance of this planetary overview is not enough to change attitudes, important and informative as it may be. On its own, it may even obscure the need for radical change in all of us and fail to challenge the presuppositions behind the "business as usual" and "at all costs" conduct of major world economies. To a very limited extent, the visible effects of passing one planetary boundary, that of climate change, have begun to influence global political and economic policies. But prevailing cultural norms, implicitly supported by pervasive mental and religious categories, ensure that we remain almost impervious to its practical and personal demands on us.

One important reason for this is that, like the Romanized Christian Empire, we regard all Earth's resources as potential sources of increased monetary wealth. This conviction is all the more powerful for now being implicit. As is

3. Rockström et al., "Planetary Boundaries."

its underlying assumption that, as a species, we are in a superior and therefore different category to all others. A corollary to that is the assumption that all other species and our shared resource base are there primarily to serve us and our "special" interests. This claim to superiority through species' distinctiveness is now generally based on perceptions of our intellectual capacities and our ability to use them to our own individual and collective advantage.

Reactions to the NGO *Earth Charter* showed that such a claim, although usually unquestioned, is bolstered culturally and religiously by the assumption that the faculty of reason and/or the possession of an immortal soul have been given to our species alone. So while our belonging to Earth in the same way as all other earthly creatures is an obvious fact at one level, our fundamental earthly oneness with them has been sidelined by analyzing it into a vertical value system.

According to this system, no less effective for being tacit, while some species are rated higher than others, we deem ourselves highest of all. Those "below" us are graded according to their usefulness to us. Lowest of all are those that inhabit the soil. Underpinning this hierarchical categorization are two presuppositions that work to the advantage of those distinguished by financial, religious, or political power. The first is that each subordinate level is not to be valued for its own sake but only in terms of its usefulness to those above it on the hierarchical scale. The second is that relationships of domination and subordination are written into human nature.

In regard to us, these presuppositions function on the basis of race, gender, wealth, and creed. In regard to other species, it means we rate them practically and economically; that is, in terms of what monetary return we may make from or with them, generally through global industrialized processes. It is taken for granted that Earth itself and its resources exist for the sake of those of us who, through economic, political, or military force, may appropriate and claim them as property: that is, with an entitlement to use them for financial wealth.

In Christian cultures, God is at the apex of this hierarchical pyramid, indeed is deemed its Creator. Earth and all other-than-human species form its base and are, therefore, assumed to be furthest from God. By definition, angels are bodiless and so closest to God. But as "earth-embodied souls," we deem ourselves next closest to "Him"; on the grounds that our souls make us "like to God." While the average churchgoer today would not use the term "paradigmatic" for this self-assessment, its religious and philosophical underpinnings have shaped and informed public and private ways of integrating different aspects of our lives into a coherent whole. Its verticality both validates and maintains a privileged place for us—or rather, for some of us—within specific social and economic systems "sanctified" as the proper political or economic order.[4]

Politically and economically this has functioned as a territorial claim: that Earth and its resources exist for a nation's use and for the financial benefit of individuals. Or, in contemporary Western economic doctrines, for the particular use and benefit of some "high-net-worth individuals" with liquid assets over a certain sum. This hierarchical presupposition is exemplified in industries built on slave labor where—in fields, mines, and factories—human beings continue to be treated like "dirt"; that is, as another resource base. Such assumptions are so deeply ingrained in the class systems of Western culture that they are taken for granted: without the need to appeal to their philosophical or religious underpinnings. This means that any recognition of our true oneness and interconnectedness, and consequent positive responses to it, have to be learned, understood, accepted, and assimilated within the different levels of our individual and collective existence.

To that end, I shall designate Earthiness as Oneness, defining it as a material, shared global state of being alive; with all life being supported by planetary resources held in common. This distinguishes it from Platonic discourse about "the One" which implies a complete lack of such physical multiplicity in that it infers a level of unity beyond that of any earthly body. In effect, this has been the intellectual basis for and the goal of a thought system that acknowledges a principle of unity beyond the earthy or physical. That is the literal meaning of the term *metaphysical*. Plato focused attention on this realm: one believed to be accessed only by the intellect or soul and inaccessible to our bodily senses. But we now know that the boundaries of our planetary realm really are "metaphysical," in the sense that they go beyond what is immediately accessible to our senses. But they remain within the physical compass of Earth's boundaries, thereby underpinning our inescapable Oneness within them and with all its creatures.

The Platonic view of unity, however, continues to support Christian hierarchies and their cultural templates where the intellectual or spiritual pursuit of "the One," whether as "the Good," or "God," is an end in itself. Pursued through rigorous intellectual and critical thinking, it is seen as needing no validity beyond the particular community that it supports and with no earthly goal or implementation in mind. Indeed, being "earthbound" is seen as an impediment to reaching "the One." A philosophical description of the mode and end of its pursuit can be found in the account of the death of Socrates, where all earthly bodily relationships (such as that with his wife and children) are considered mere distractions from continuing discussion of ideas:

4. Primavesi, *From Apocalypse to Genesis*, 88–106.

The speeches of the Phaedo, and more precisely the philosophical discourses that untie the soul from the body, take place in the cell where Socrates is sitting with his male friends during the final hours before his death. Xanthippe, his wife, has been hastily thrown out. This is not a place for women. Socrates does not want any women in the cell when he comes close to accomplishing the "living for death" announced by philosophy. Thus while waiting for the perfect, definitive untying, he attains the experience of death through a final dialogue about his own death.[5]

In Christian circles influenced by Platonism, Denys the Areopagite coined the term *hierarchia* or "sacred order" to describe the concept of working out a cosmic pattern of government whose aim is "the greatest possible assimilation and union with God."[6] While this does not exclude a perception of our bodily Oneness within the community of life on earth, it focuses attention on the incorporeal union between (implied) low, middle, and high orders of being that correspond to graded stages of divine knowledge and spiritual activity leading beyond this material world. The basic Platonic structure of thought is intended to move us "upward" toward the One (God) by going beyond earthly embodiedness. Reality is perceived as being arranged in graded vertical levels that mediate and relate to one another as subordinate hierarchies linked through a cosmic sympathy that embraces the whole; albeit in an outward *downward* movement of progressively diminishing radiation from God.

This underlying conceptual verticality and the human order based on it still finds its fullest material expression in Roman Catholic and Orthodox ecclesiastical hierarchies, ministries, liturgies, and architecture. In these, primacy is given to the sanctuary and to those men entitled to minister from within it. Implicitly, this physical "barrier" between sacred and profane exemplifies the continuing reluctance within church hierarchies to ordain women.[7] Like Xanthippe, they are assumed to be tied to corporeal bonds that bind the soul to earth, keeping it from its true home "above." The wider cultural impact of such paradigms or vertical mental patterns that give us (or rather some of us) a privileged position not only on Earth but within the Universe, was demonstrated in the reaction to Galileo's discovery of Earth's true place in our solar system: a discovery that, by implication, challenged our hitherto unquestioned superior role and place within it.

This conjunction of cultural and religious hierarchicalism supported the assumption (for that is what it was) that God had created a universe in

5. Cavarero, *In Spite of Plato*, 28–29.

6. Primavesi, *From Apocalypse to Genesis*, 89.

7. Ibid., 90.

which the Sun and other planets revolved around Earth: and so around us. Three centuries later, science apparently triumphed when Galileo had been vindicated and our true place within the solar system, that is, within the planetary community of life, was established. In Darwin's words, we could now see ourselves as lineal descendants of previous forms of life:

> There is grandeur in this view of life, with its several powers, having been originally breathed into a few forms or into one; and that, whilst this planet has gone cycling on (around the Sun) according to a fixed law of gravity, from so simple a beginning endless forms most beautiful and most wonderful have been, and are being, evolved.[8]

However, the "grandeur" of this view of the oneness of earthly life was initially resisted by some as scientific heresy, as well as by those culturally and religiously disposed to discern and dismiss its implications for any claim to special status for our species. Regrettably, as I found with the responses to the *Earth Charter*, those implications are still rejected by some of us precisely on those grounds. Generally speaking, they are given token acceptance—and then ignored. So our arrogated right to ownership and to sole use of Earth's planetary resources is implicitly upheld. We continue to behave as if we alone (or more accurately, some of us) have a divine or civil right to them as our property; and so continue to claim the use of them for our own benefit and pleasure, whatever the destructive cost to other living creatures.

In effect, this has meant that, unlike the Galatians, no war has been declared against them. But conflicting interhuman claims to Earth's resources have led to the habitats of other-than-human species being destroyed and/or their lives endangered; some to the point of extinction. No bombs are dropped directly on the Amazon rainforest. Indirectly, the global mindset that sees its particular resources as exploitable for monetary gain is indirectly destroying the lives of all inhabitants, human and other-than-human, who depend on them.

The fact that we *know* how these destructive processes work distances us from fourth-century Rome. Officially, with some notable exceptions, Christians now also appear to have distanced themselves from any need to either justify or condemn this on religious grounds: that is, as being compatible or incompatible with Jesus's teaching. The glaring disparity between them was a real issue in fourth-century Roman Christianity and was coped with in some instructive ways:

8. Darwin, *The Origin of Species*, 459–60.

> Splendor was the key term in the definition of wealth. Splendor
> assumed income. But the practice of splendor gave little thought
> to financial matters in themselves. Rather, it had everything to
> do with how one looked, how one dressed, how one ate, how one
> travelled, and, last but not least, how often one bathed. Wealth
> sheathed the bodies of the rich with a set of unmistakable signals
> of prosperity and good fortune.[9]

So for educated, wealthy Christians such as Paulinus of Nola a retreat from
splendor was seen as essential. He achieved it—in his own eyes—by taking
apart and inverting at every point the social semiotics of the fourth-century
rich. In describing himself and his fellow ascetics, he left a memorable image
of "poverty" as "anti-wealth"; not as "unwealth." He and a group of men with
whom he identified no longer lived in great villas but in cramped cells and in
close contact with the drab masses of the poor. They ate plain food and drank
a minimum of wine from earthenware and wooden vessels. Above all, they
were enveloped in the dull smell of the underbathed. This, says Brown, was the
sure mark of poverty in the ancient world. (And still is.)

Paulinus's notion of poverty as anti-wealth was so cogent to his contemporaries because, says Brown, it was grounded in intimate identification with
the person of Christ. What Christ was this? He was, says Brown, very much
the Christ of a particular generation. One might even say that he was a Christ
whose image was calculated to resonate with Christians of a particular class
faced by the dilemma of a person who was at times weak and helpless. Yet, for
Christians after Nicaea, a Christ who was also the "fullness of divinity." For
Ambrose and then for Paulinus, he was very much a "late Roman Christ"; one
whose humility was all the more stunning because it was based on a conscious
act of self-effacement on the part of the majestic God whom he continued
to be. The Christ of Paulinus was poor because he was a God who had hidden his *splendor* (but retained it) through a splendid act of self-effacement or
humility:

> "Humility" and "humble" are words to which Paulinus returns
> incessantly when speaking of Christ. And by "humble" Paulinus
> means a posture to the world that was defined in more sharply
> social terms than can be conveyed by the sentimental modern as-
> sociations of the word: to be "humble" in the later Roman Empire
> was to be, quite bluntly, "unimportant."[10]

9. Brown, *Through the Eye of a Needle*, 220.
10. Ibid., 222.

In such a way, Brown concludes, a converted aristocrat and his circle, who had carefully dismantled themselves of the strident denotations by which persons of wealth, power, and status had stood out in the late Roman world, faced society "as the bearers of a Christ equally shorn—but only for the time being—of his majesty."[11]

"Only for the time being." Herein lies the key to the notion of wealth in fourth-century Rome: as a spiritual exchange by which wealth on earth became treasure in heaven. For Paulinus, "worldly" wealth that stood for all that was most brittle in this world, most unspiritual, most stubbornly rebellious to the will of God, could be transmuted through acts of pious giving to the poor into all that was most glittering and glorious in heaven. This "spiritual exchange" meant that base, earthly wealth joined the distant purity of the heavens. Feeding the poor was not simply an act of charity on earth: it mirrored heaven on earth. Ultimately the story of the Rich Young man did not obsess Paulinus as much as did the story of Dives and Lazarus. If only, Paulinus insists, Dives had stopped to look at Lazarus and pressed some alms into his hand, he would not have been buried in hell.[12]

> All of this was welcomed by landowners. No product of the wild or of cultivated land was shown in its own right. All of nature was presented only as if it were to be "offered up" to the dominus, the owner of the estate—preferably by ranks of neatly dressed and deferential peasants. The numinous bounty of the land was undeniable. But it had, as it were, been tilted toward human owners. It existed only to be given to the lords of the land.[13]

The above account is a mere outline of Brown's masterly study of wealth, poverty and the gap between the rich and the poor in the Roman Empire of the fourth century CE. But it reveals salient attitudes to ownership of the Earth and its resources that strike a very contemporary note. It shows how the desacralization of the land has involved a transfer of the notion of fruitfulness from the land and its resources to what human beings make of it and get from it. And by doing so, implicitly and explicitly grants them full license to make the most monetary profit possible from that fruitfulness. This egocentric, utilitarian attitude that values Earth in human terms has had lasting effects not only on our shared planetary resources but on us.

In the following chapters this historic trajectory will be traced in some detail. Here I shall finish by simply stating that when and where the value of

11. Ibid., 223.

12. Ibid., 224–38.

13. Ibid., 239.

nature is assessed primarily in monetary terms, we forfeit any entitlement to the fundamental sense of well-being that is one of Earth's greatest gifts to us and to all living beings. This relies on a sense of the intrinsic value of the other-than-human world, based religiously on the non-hierarchical implications of the biblical tenets that state:

> God saw all that was made; and it was very good;
>
> God sent the groundling away . . . to serve the Earth from which it was taken.[14]

---

14. Gen 1:31; 3:23 translated by Korsak, *At the Start*, 4, 11.

2

Disdained Earth

Earth I am, it is most trew; disdain me not, for soe are you.

This inscription appears on a 1672 tin-glazed earthenware hand-warmer in the form of a book found in the Ashmolean Museum in Oxford. Even in the seventeenth century, this potter discerned how humans disdain the earth "from which we were taken" (Gen 3:23); and on which our lives depend. So the inscription remains as relevant and challenging as when it was first written and read. Our continuing disdainful attitudes to our shared earthiness are now evident in the degradation through human appropriation and exploitation of Earth's rivers, soil, forests, seas, air, skies, and life forms on a global scale. A contemporary egregious example is the expansion and development of Canada's tar sands industry into other countries; extracting shale oil from the ground with dire and immediate effects on the surrounding land, its forests, its waters, its atmosphere, its other-than-human species, and its people. Presently there are calls for permits to allow oil exploration in the Arctic Ocean. Yet we have the evidence that such major projects inevitably result in contamination of the local, continental, and ultimately global environment and atmosphere.

This is happening after we have seen Earth from space; seen it as a whole constituted by its land, water, oceans, atmosphere, and inhabitants. And it continues to happen even though we have measured and analyzed (with increasing detail and accuracy) the effects of human industries and lifestyles on the lives, habitats, and potential future of all those creatures, including ourselves, who are entirely reliant on the support of Earth's unique life-resources. If this does not demonstrate human disdain for the Earth, then what does? The seventeenth-century craftsman did not "know" Earth as we do today. Yet in spite of our increased knowledge, within Western culture there is little evidence of increased respect for it. Those who now take its exploitation as a human right disdain it as surely as did any of those addressed by that potter.

The cultural role played in this desacralization of the natural world is increasingly evident to those individuals and groups who, in partnership with indigenous peoples, work for the conservation of global wildlife and resources. Their collective efforts are a source of hope at a time when the growth and use of technologies that debase Earth and its complex resource base for short-term commercial use and financial gain claim most media attention. This neither acknowledges nor respects the limits of planetary resources on which all its past and present inhabitants have drawn and which continue to be needed to support new life.

In contrast to this attitude, Andrew Balmford, Professor of Conservation at the University of Cambridge, draws much-needed attention to people and places where conservation efforts are improving things. He cites a successful campaign in Assam to save the large Indian rhino, one of the rarest animals on the planet. Almost as marvelous as the creatures themselves, he says, is the paradox of their persistence. They and other endangered species have been allowed to flourish in a region with a long history of bloody civil unrest, and in a park surrounded by more than 70,000 people. Their household incomes are often less than US $10 a month, whereas a rhino poacher can earn far more in one night. So how is this success possible?

Balmford gives two overwhelming reasons. One is the dedication and bravery of hundreds of conservation professionals working with and within the local populations. They repair roads and camps; keep the jeeps, boats, and working elephants in running order; carry out managed burns to hold the growth of grassland trees in check; and undertake annual censuses of the park's residents. Above all, they patrol for poachers. More broadly, local people's respect for these big and distinctly dangerous creatures is manifest in their quite extraordinary tolerance of the damage they cause. The human costs of living so closely with large animals are very significant: they eat crops, damage fields, flatten homes, attack livestock, and even kill and injure people.

Even more striking, says Balmford, is the Indian peoples' general acceptance of this. He compares it with the appearance not long ago of the first wild bear seen in Germany since 1835. It lasted only a few weeks before accusations of killing sheep (not to mention raiding a rabbit hutch) led to its being shot dead. Here in Britain, supported by a majority of dairy farmers, the government tried to sanction a badger cull on the grounds that the badgers infect commercial cattle herds with tuberculosis. Public reaction against the cull is such that, for now, the policy has been abandoned.[1]

This Western cultural disrespect for indigenous species persists even as we grow in understanding of how sharing planetary resources has made possible the evolution of all Earth's present lifeforms, including our own, over billions of years. This is a real challenge for us today: to act out of our growing knowledge of Earth's species' evolution and acknowledge our true place among them. For we know that we are but one amid tens of millions inhabiting this planet; all of whom are dependent on the same resources that we exploit.

We are also beginning to discern, albeit reluctantly, the consequences for all species, including our own, if we refuse to accept the implications of this shared dependence. Before examining some of the reasons for this refusal in more detail, as well as their effects on ourselves and some positive reactions to them, I shall consider briefly two recent, groundbreaking insights that demonstrate our belonging within the community of life on Earth—and nowhere else. Both concern our bodies but in different ways.

Firstly, scientists have discovered that we share with other earthly life forms genetic systems and mutations within organisms, together with different inheritance patterns in them. These inherited traits have been essential to our evolution as a species—as just one among countless others. As of now, this is the only planet we know of on which this irresistible march of evolutionary processes, outcomes and energy forces operate to this end. Therefore we owe our very existence to the fact that, as Nils Eldredge observes:

> From the microscopic to the global, Earth is truly "a living" system, a globally pulsing amalgam of organisms and the physical "inanimate" world. . . . We owe the five fingers on our hands not to novel evolutionary events a million years ago on the African savannahs, but rather as a holdover from the original complement of five digits on the forefoot of the earliest land vertebrates (tetrapods) who evolved some 370 million years ago.[2]

Secondly, such scientific affirmation of our shared evolving earthiness is endorsed by the experience of exploring space. For this has clearly demonstrated our inability to survive without Earth's atmosphere. To go beyond it and remain alive, we must take it with us: together with enough earthly food and water

1. Balmford, *Wild Hope*, 19–33.
2. Margulis and Sagan, *What Is Life?*, 9.

to sustain us. Journeying beyond earth's gravitational bounds has given us a view of our planetary home as one with lifeforms and an atmosphere unique to it within the known universe. Seeing it from this perspective reinforces the truth that we belong here and nowhere else; that Earth is essential to our survival as a species. Our lives are only possible because of mutual, essential interactions between us, its other inhabitants, and its resources. This deepening understanding of our earthiness has been acquired in ways undreamt of by a seventeenth-century craftsman and serves to reinforce his insight.

But have our attitudes to Earth or our own earthiness changed since his lifetime? Has our disdain for it lessened as a result of all this information? If anything, there seems now to be a greater reluctance, a stronger resistance to accepting that, as his artifact proclaims, we are made from, sustained by and identified materially with Earth; both in life and in death. Reasons for this reluctance will be explored in some detail. Briefly here, they can be seen to fall into two closely related but distinct mental categories. The first is that of human self-image, our self-image as a species. For, as Keith Thomas remarks, it is impossible to disentangle what the people of the past thought about plants and animals from what they thought about themselves.[3] And that still holds true, although the language we use to convey our thoughts may be very different.

In Western developed cultures, when thinking and speaking about ourselves we draw on socially accepted distinctions between the "material world" and the "immaterial." This assumes that the world consists of two different kinds of things; material bodies and immaterial minds. They are represented by various categories of body/mind dualities largely biased in favor of "mind"; of the "immaterial." In everyday discourse, this implicit bias is often taken literally and in some instances explicitly supports "disdain" for our earthy, bodily materialness. "Ideas" are discussed and promoted above "feelings"; as if the former exist apart from the body of the person advocating, rejecting or pursuing them. The account of Socrates's death in the previous chapter illustrates this perfectly.

The second closely related reason for disdaining Earth is our image of it as a totally material "body." Images are always in dialogue with action and different types of behavior are linked to those of language. When affirming different forms of human oneness we may look at each other, join hands and sing together. But the unspoken belief that what we cannot see, hear or touch also exists, colors our attitudes to the material realm, and gives it an immaterial, numinous character as well. So while the visible, material existence of the body of our planet is normally seen as its defining characteristic, scientific advances make us increasingly aware that Earth, and we its creatures, exist

3. Thomas, *Man and the Natural World*, 16.

only by virtue of the fact that its material composition, mobility and chang-ing seasons are affected by immaterial forces invisible to human eyes, such as gravity. And that these also affect us.

A basic sameness between our self-image and our Earth-image is emerg-ing that highlights Earth as the "mother" or substance of our human material-ity. This function was, of course, also attributed to Hesiod's Gaia. But she was effectively desacralized by being made subordinate to human strength: a self-image based on a belief in a divinely granted ability to transcend our physical limitations. For as the potter discerned, we draw rather different conclusions from the knowledge that both Gaia and ourselves are regulated by "immate-rial" forces.

In regard to Earth, while we now know that previously invisible dyna-misms determine its journey through space, we have long been aware that other factors, such as the seasonal and daily rhythms of the sun and moon, are vital to its mode of existence and so also to our own. In pre-scientific hu-man communities such control over material substances, whether planetary or personal, was presumed to be exercised by non-material mythic divinities such as Athena, Thor, Krishna; or by an invisible religious deity. And it may be argued that our knowledge of how this control is exercised has simply been extended and deepened to encompass similar "immaterial" forces: energies and entities like gravity, photons, neutrinos, etc. The important point is that in whatever form we imagine them or represent them, we believe them to exercise an immaterial power over Earth and ourselves that is invisible to us and extends beyond our immediate material world.

A variation on this perception directly affects our presuppositions about our relationships with and within Earth, whether or not we are aware of it. The smart move here has been from an abstraction, "life," (found in everything from microbes to trees to elephants) to "intelligent information processing"; that is, to analyses of the immaterial, invisible influences that affect our mate-rial bodies. These analyses have been acclaimed as the work of "great minds," usually those of rationally and economically privileged, scientifically literate and conventionally male human beings. On the basis of their work, decisions are made that drive our own lives and conduct in certain directions and not others. And those decisions have affected and continue to affect not only our-selves but all other-than-human creatures and our shared environments.

What conclusions have they drawn about the relationship between Earth and us? In 1610, scientist Johannes Kepler drew a religious conclusion echoing that of Ignatius of Loyola in the previous century: that "all things have been made [by God] for man." However Galileo, Kepler's contemporary, rejected this on the grounds that such an idea was simply an unthinking manifestation of human presumption. Another of Galileo's contemporaries, Descartes, also rejected this view on grounds that have a more contemporary scientific resonance. Although, he said, it may be a pious thought to believe that God made all things for us, and that this may incite us to greater gratitude and love toward him; and although in some sense it may even be true, since there is no created thing of which we cannot make some use [!]; if only that of exercising our mind in considering it and honoring God on account of it:

> Yet it is by no means probable that all things were created for us in this way that God had no other end in their creation; and this supposition would be plainly ridiculous and inept in physical reasoning, for we do not doubt but that many things exist, or formerly existed and have now ceased to be, which were never seen or known by man, and were never of use to him.[4]

However, although Descartes didn't draw Kepler's conclusion from distinctions between human and all other earthly bodies, he defined those distinctions in ways that have had a profound impact on our self-image and are largely still taken for granted in Western societies today. He argued from "the truth" [sic] that, "*I think, hence I am*," to the conclusion that the human mind is wholly distinct from and exists independently from the body:

> I thence concluded that "I" was a substance whose whole essence or nature consists only in thinking, and which, that it may exist, has need of no place, nor is dependent on any material thing: so that "I," that is to say, the mind by which I am what I am, is wholly distinct from the body and is even more easily known than the latter, and is such, that although the latter were not, it would still continue to be all that it is.[5]

This concept of mind as the defining human characteristic that enables us to think *without body* makes a distinction between one and the other in ways which elevate the mind by not only supposing it to be independent of the body but capable of existing outside it. Such Cartesian idealism underpins the contemporary Anthropic Principle, which connects (human) "mind" and our capacity to observe and understand what happens in the world with our unique status here as "observers."[6] However and whenever proposed or argued for, such a presumed relationship between a conceptualized, immaterial "mind" and an earthly material body functions to elevate us to a unique

4. Descartes, *A Discourse on Method*, 213.
5. Ibid., xix.
6. Primavesi, *Gaia's Gift*, 32–34; 137.

status and position in relationship to all other species: and to the Earth they and we inhabit. By making the power of thought supposedly independent of any material substance, it elevates "mind over matter." The human "mind" becomes an implied invisible force in control of earthly matter. This lays bare and underlies the force of our "mental categories."

A moment's reflection on a temporary illness during which a person may be incapable of thought because of a lack of blood flow to the brain should dispel any Cartesian assumptions about mind being "wholly distinct from body." However, these assumptions are commonplace and continue to have deleterious effects on the prevailing cultural and educational human self-image and, by default, on our relationship with Earth. Their influence exemplifies what Gregory Bateson called the phenomenon of *habit formation*. This identifies ideas that survive repeated use and puts them in a more or less separate category where they are so taken for granted that they become axiomatic assumptions on which no thinking-time or effort need to be wasted. This allows the more flexible parts of the mind to engage on newer or more pressing matters. Frequency of use guarantees their survival and this survival is further promoted by the fact that habit formation tends to remove these ideas from the field of critical inspection.[7]

In fact, ideas that consistently elevate mind over body, the immaterial over the material (and consequently justify putting our perceived interests over those of all other earthly species and habitats) not only persist to this day but have existed in one form or another since well before the seventeenth century. One such is Plato's injunction to philosophers, epitomized in the death of Socrates: "[U]ntie the soul from the body . . . by contemplating truth, the divine and what is not appearance, and being nurtured by it."[8]

This human self-image has not only profoundly affected Christian teaching on the immortality of the soul and the mortal earthiness of the body, with religious and cultural priority given to the former. Since the Romanization of Western Christianity, this deadly distinction remains culturally entangled with prevailing images of Earth: rendering it an almost redundant adjunct to human history. It assumes, indeed teaches, that while here "we have no lasting city," our "real" home is heaven. In such ways "salvation economics" trades our mortal earthly life for an immortal one; calibrated on accumulating and exchanging worldly riches for heavenly "futures."

These mental religious categories (for they have no existence outside the mind) are in stark contrast to those that Balmford discerns as the second reason for why the local Assamese people put up with the human costs of living

7. Bateson, *Steps to an Ecology of Mind*, 499f.
8. Plato, *Phaedo* 84a-b, translated by Cavarero, *In Spite of Plato*, 11.

so closely with large, destructive, and life-threatening animals like the rhino. Everyone he asked about this, he says, attributes it to firmly held religious beliefs regarding the rights of other creatures.

> While not many people go as far as those Jains who sweep the floor in front of them to avoid treading on insects, for most Hindus and Buddhists (which in practice means most Indians) all animals are divine. The great God Ganesh has an elephant head. Other animals too are the living incarnations of deities. . . . And if they destroy the crops anyway? Then we say to them, "Father, please, go away."[9]

Balmford does not underestimate the cost to the human population of such an attitude, especially in communities characterized by overwhelming human poverty. But an enduring theme emerging from the study of our attitudes to earthiness that will be directly addressed in the following chapters is Western cultures' defining "riches" solely in terms of monetary wealth: accumulated up to now through the possession of land and its produce as property. This now goes beyond our colonizing Earth to the notion of our being able to "conquer space" and "colonize" Mars.

Up to now, this self-understanding has manifested itself culturally and practically in an important distinction *within* the human self-image; one that aligns the powers of creativity, rationality, and spirituality with the male principle and the virtues of receptivity and materiality with the female. During and after the seventeenth century, when the idea of male supremacy in conception was taken as self-evident, women and children, together with the Earth and its fruits, were all seen to be and were treated as the property of men, their bodies to be used for generating material human bodies and/or wealth. As a central tenet of civil law and government, the idea of property not only rationalized proprietorial attitudes towards women, land, its creatures and its resources. It also served as a political argument for colonization as a process of appropriating lands, indigenous peoples, and resources by distinguishing between the rights and duties of both colonizers and colonized.

In this regard, the significance of one of the most important documents underlying *The Founders' Constitution of the United States*, John Locke's 1689 *Two Treatises of Government* (especially Chapters V and VI in the Second Treatise headed: "*Of Property*") cannot be overestimated. A powerful external token of their basic tenets followed inexorably in the extinctions of buffalo, carrier pigeons, and other indigenous species.

The next chapter will look closely at these documents for, according to the present editors of the American *Founders' Constitution*, they "present

9. Balmford, *Wild Hope*, 35–36.

arguments of yesteryear put forward by men who prided themselves on their reasonableness." They are worth reexamining, say the editors, because they are "a recurring point of reference," a "legitimation of further developments." This (apparently) enabled them to pursue arguments (untainted by feelings, emotion, or sensitivity) that justified the dispossession and disenfranchisement of the native peoples and the appropriation of their land. In other words, they reflect ideas and opinions that remain largely unquestioned and habitually held in Western culture today. This is the case even though they originated at a time when, in the editors' words:

> America might better be seen as a collection of highly diverse, discrete settlements, more intimately acquainted with England than with one another, more closely tied to their ancestral home (three months' sea voyage away) than to their neighbors.[10]

10. Kurland and Lerner, *The Founders' Constitution*, 2, 4.

3

Appropriated Earth

While there are different theories concerning the origins of private property, it is certain that the first forms arose in the late eighth century BCE, gaining ground in Greece and in the whole of the ancient Near East. It is also certain that money originated around the same time (not yet in the form of coins).[1]

It is no coincidence that Duchrow and Hinkelammert speak of the first forms of private property in terms of "gaining ground." For the most visible, material symbol of the ownership of property was and remains the staking out, fencing off or building of walls around "ground" that had once been common land, that is, common "property." The basic referent of "property" continues to be a piece of earth and all its other-than-human inhabitants; the whole legally possessed by an individual person or group to use or dispose of at will. This concept confronts us daily in high street windows where the "properties" displayed for sale are houses or commercial buildings situated on particular plots of land. They include hereditary estates, old or newly built dwellings, flats or factories; all there to be sold by qualified agents on behalf of their owners. The terms of sale specify their legal right to sell and that of prospective owners to buy. Then the practical and legal ramifications of a purchase must be dealt

---

1. Duchrow and Hinkelammert, *Property for People, Not for Profit*, 5.

with after its monetary value is agreed. Indeed the latter is usually the overriding consideration for both parties.

This is so "normal" a transaction that we simply take it for granted. Yet only once in Earth's history (as far as we know) has a single species tried to live in defiance of the fact that the boundaries of the "planetary playing field" and the resources it contains exist to foster life for all members of the Earth community. And that therefore, according to species type, by sharing those resources they foster life for more than the immediate members of their own species. An obvious example is the bee that collects nectar for its own hive and in doing so, pollinates plants whose fruits feed members of other species. Basic to this interspecies resource sharing are Earth's water, air, sunlight, soil, oceans, stratospheric ozone, biogeochemical nitrogen, and phosphorus. They foster life for the grasses, for the grasshopper that feeds on them, for the bird that feeds on the grasshopper, for the fox that feeds on the bird, for the crows that feed on the dead fox.

Whatever "chain of being" one examines, it leads to the conclusion that as a species, our claim to "own" Earth's resources and to use them for our monetary profit, often to the detriment of the good of the whole, is not only evidence of a presumed isolation from the lives of all other species. It also blinds us to the nature of the planetary "commons" within which we belong and on which all depend. And to the truth that the effects of our actions are steadily destroying that shared life support system.

On investigation, it has become clear that such disdain for Earth's systems, processes, and resources relies on some presuppositions already mentioned: that the Universe revolves around Earth and, that as we are at the center of Earth, it revolves around us. In other words, that Earth was "made" for us to claim and use for our sole benefit. Supported by religion, philosophy, and civil law, this concept of human supremacy slowly became the "fact" of our ownership of property. After the Romanization of Christianity this presupposition gained ground until it became standard practice to assess land, its other-than-human beings, and its resources in terms of human claims to entitlement. Earth and its creatures were there to be bartered, "translated" into monetary terms and, through this process, desacralized: detached from any relationship with the divine.

For the general public, the process of monetization has been applied largely to one type of property—to buildings used for a variety of purposes surrounded by large or small areas of land. This now serves as a template for all transactions dependent on monetary exchanges to transfer ownership of some kind from one person or group of persons to another. During the transfer disputes may arise as to whether specified items of property are worth less or more than is being asked for them: which requires legal advice. A less immediately material kind of possession, the ownership of ideas, is treated as intellectual "property" and sold as such. This may involve claims to copyright or the lodging of patents, for example, all supervised by the proper authorities in order to safeguard reputations; or more importantly, any future monetary return on the ideas in question. All these transactions require interlocking networks of landowners, lawyers, estate agents, bankers, businessmen, surveyors, accountants, auctioneers, property developers, and different "stock" exchanges. Driving the whole process, on both sides, is a competition to get the best monetary return for buyer or seller.

In seventeenth-century England such property exchanges were dominated by the landed gentry. A rather less obvious type of property led John Locke to write the *Two Treatises of Government*. This was the possession of freeholds and "liberties" such as a university fellowship, a commission in the Army or Navy, or a benefice in the Church. These too were considered the "property" of their owners. The experience of the political and religious upheavals of the seventeenth century and in particular, Cromwell's and James II's attacks on these institutions, had added limpet-like strength to men's attachment to such possessions. In an England littered with these myriad marks of status, of possession, of profit, it was men only who could and did possess them: as stewards of "hundreds," precentors of cathedrals or beadles of corporations:

> Usually these offices were held for life and they all enjoyed standing and status within the community they adorned; most of them carried a vote. Such freeholds bred independence, truculence, a willingness to fight and litigate that bordered on neurosis; and yet when they conglomerated, as in the universities, the cathedral cities and the Parliamentary boroughs, they could build up into formidable heaps of political influence. If Britain was ever to enjoy political peace, it was necessary to harmonize their interests with those of the national government. . . . These men, with the landowners and merchants, great or small, were the men of property for whom John Locke wrote his "Two Treatises."[2]

This glimpse of the background to Locke's writings and the situation they addressed not only gives us clues to some accepted seventeenth-century uses of the term "property" and some of its effects on the men holding it. It also discloses major presuppositions behind the term that continue to this day. Foremost among these is the self-image of an "owner": an independent-minded, aggressive, politically influential man. This image was supported by the

2. Plumb, *The Growth of Political Stability in England 1675–1725*, 27–28.

myriad marks of status and income attached to an estate, a freehold, an office of State, a benefice of the Church, or a university fellowship. Some of these vested interests could be valued in monetary terms and so, in some instances, the influence attached to them could be sold. Then as now, an individual or group controls the use, assets, potential sale and also the right to destroy a legally owned property if he or they so choose. Disdain or appreciation for the earth on which a property is based remains proportionate to the money, influence or market value it brings with it: rather than its fostering of life in all its forms. In other words, it becomes and is treated as a commercial commodity.

This commercial value, together with the social and cultural image of power and influence attached to property and to those who own it, still holds good. Habitually, it denotes a relationship of control by the owner over the property's present state and future potential, either for growth, monetary exchange, the development of assets or their destruction. The underlying presupposition about the role of a property owner is that his control is exercised primarily and legitimately on his authority and in his own interests. And that his status and influence, over and against that of others, is closely bound up with the size and monetary value of the property. At the global level, this now characterizes human attitudes to Earth. Rather than seeing ourselves as belonging to Earth, we presume it belongs to us, appropriating it for our use and financial benefit.

Bearing all this in mind, I want to look in some detail at certain statements about property in Locke's *Second Treatise of Government* (1689), conscious that it has had a profound effect on the American Founding Fathers and on the process of colonization worldwide. In terms of its mental categorizations, it remains, as we saw, "a recurring point of reference" and "a legitimation of further developments." So while the treatise is clearly the product of a particular moment in English history, it can also be read as a summation of previous ideas and a reference point for recurring ideas that remain widely held to this day. As we shall see, they still undergird presuppositions about our relationship with Earth, its resources and its creatures. So it is essential to examine them in the light of their present effects and of developments in our understanding of that relationship.

Locke's own guiding presupposition was a belief in a divine order that, in his view, underlay the relationship between "Men" and "Earth." (I shall stay with Locke's use of "Men" as representing all humanity). As a Christian, he based his description of this divinely ordained relationship on one enshrined in the Bible, one he could presuppose his readers took for granted. A pre-Christian, indeed pre-biblical attempt to describe this divine order had been made in Hesiod's poem *Works and Days*. There the poet focused on the farmer's life as archetype of the relationship between Men and Earth. A major difference between these two authors was, of course, that for Hesiod, "Earth" herself, Demeter (Gaia), was part of the "divine" order controlling the fruitfulness of earthly life and with it, human life. She was one of the "First Gods":

> Pray to Zeus-Under-Earth and to Demeter the Holy
> That the sacred corn of Demeter be heavy when ready for harvest.[3]

Locke, however, in Chapter 2 of *The Second Treatise*, focused on the ownership of "property" as the archetypal relationship between us and God and, by divine appointment so to speak, between Men and Earth. He named Men as the product of divine "workmanship" and therefore God's "property." This meant, he said, that they are under God's control: living by his order and at his pleasure; doing his business while sharing in one Community of Nature and using "inferior Creatures" to that end:

> For Men being all the Workmanship of one Omnipotent and infinitely wise Maker, sent into the World by his order and about his business, they are his Property, whose Workmanship they are, made to last during his, not one another's Pleasure. And being furnished with like Faculties, sharing all in one Community of Nature, there cannot be any such Subordination among us, that may Authorize us to destroy one another, as if we were made for one another's uses, as the inferior Creatures are for ours.[4]

The phrase "by his order and about his business" pretty well still defines, in western cultures, the relationship between a proprietor and a person, place or "inferior creatures" owned by, or acknowledged as his property. Instead, Locke uses the template of Creator and Proprietor to outline and characterize our relationship with God, our "omnipotent and infinitely wise Maker." And he presumes that as His proxies, this also characterizes our relationship with Earth. As such, we cannot legitimately destroy one another: for we were made with "like faculties" and for divine, not human use. We may, however, own or destroy those without those faculties, that is, "the inferior Creatures" who may be used as our property and, if we wish, may be destroyed by us. He takes for granted our proprietorship of the land itself and its resources and therefore, our right to use and destroy it. Implicitly, this devalues earth and its "inferior" Creatures in our favor. A far cry from the beliefs held by the people of Assam and their often costly acceptance of their fellow creatures referred to in Chapter 2.

3. Nelson, *God and the Land*, 21, 46–48, 96, 104.
4. Laslett, *Locke*, 271.

Instead, defining "Men" in terms of a role normally attributed to God implies their being divinely elevated above all Earth creatures within "the one Community of Nature." It puts them at the apex of a lineage based on owner-ship of Earth; with that as "property" handed down to "Men"; or more precise-ly to some of them, as we shall see. And certainly not to "inferior Creatures." This archetypal verticality and hierarchical self-image puts humans above all other creatures and gives them the right to own them as "property" and to use them and the Earth for their own purposes.

How does Locke legitimate this right? By pointing to that "Faculty" which, in his estimation, sets Men above all other creatures:

> God, who hath given the World to Men in common, hath also given them reason to make use of it to the best advantage of Life, and convenience. The Earth, and all that is therein, is given to Men for the Support and Comfort of their being.[5]

The God-given faculty of reason, Locke argues, is the basis for Men's right to use the World to their own advantage, for their own support and comfort. Locke goes on to elevate the use of "Reason" to the status of a divine com-mand to "subdue" the Earth. The *raison d'etre* for Earth's existence as Men's property is to use and improve it by their labor and for their sole advantage. Furthermore, the "Title" (of proprietor) is given to Men in exchange for their obedience to the command of God to subdue, till, and sow any particular part acquired as property:

> God and his Reason commanded him to subdue the Earth, i.e., improve it for the benefit of Life, and therein lay out something upon it that was his own, his labour. He that in obedience to this Command of God, subdued, tilled and sowed any part of it, there-by annexed to it some thing that was his Property, which another had no Title to, nor could without injury take from him.[6]

Locke's claim that we obey God by using our reason to subdue the Earth and make it Men's property brings together a particularly powerful and enduring Christian self-image with an equally powerful Earth image. It relates one to the other by the conjunction of divine "Reason" with human "reason." This mental category (in every sense) decisively differentiates "Men" from "Earth" and from all "inferior Creatures." At the same time it gives Men the right to use force to subdue and use them for their own "reasonable" purposes. "Rea-son" is invoked as a divine attribute and as an immaterial gift to the human

5. Ibid., 286.
6. Ibid., 291.

material body alone. It legitimates Men's possession of Earth; to own and to use for their personal benefit. This ownership is modeled on the relationship between the faculty of reason as a controlling force and the human body. Just as reason "owns," controls, or has property in the body, so too Man's labor, the work of his hands and its fruits remain properly "his" property:

> Though the Earth, and all inferior Creatures be common to all Men, yet every Man has a Property in his own Person. This no Body has any Right to but himself. The Labour of his Body and the Work of his hands, we may say, are properly his.[7]

The logic of this argument is that as human reason, or mind, owns the human body by right as its property, so the human faculty of reason owns Earth's body. And so too the fruits of the labor of a Man's body and the work of his hands are his by right. They, however, are presumed to be controlled and owned by his reason, for Reason has property both in the body and in the bodily work that brings forth fruit from the Earth for the comfort and support of human bodies.

What exactly does Locke mean here by "reason"? In *An Essay Concerning Human Understanding*, published in 1690, he acknowledges that it has various significations or meanings and then highlights the one that in his view distinguishes "Man" from all other creatures:

> [Reason] stands for a faculty in man, that faculty whereby man is supposed to be distinguished from beasts, and wherein it is evident he much surpasses them. . . . Sense and intuition reach but a very little way. The greatest part of our knowledge rests upon deductions and intermediate ideas; and in those cases where we are fain to substitute assent instead of knowledge, and take propositions for true, without being certain they are so, we have need to find out, examine, and compare the grounds of their probability. In both these cases, the faculty which finds out the means and rightly applies them, to discover certainty in the one, and probability in the other, is that which we call reason.[8]

This is the basis on which I am examining his propositions. It is also the basis on which I conclude that he is right in saying that when God "gave" the world to Men he also gave them reason so that they could make use of it to the best advantage. But it also reasonable, indeed necessary to challenge his conclusion that because this (supposedly) distinguishes us from "the inferior Creatures" and clearly allows us to surpass them in certain ways, we may use them for

7. Ibid., 289.
8. Locke, *An Essay Concerning Human Understanding*, 415–16.

our purposes: that is, solely to our advantage and irrespective of theirs. This Lockean argument relies on a divine vertical order in which we are the Workmanship of one infinitely wise God who, furnishing us with a faculty, Reason, like to his own, entitles us to use Earth and its other-than-human creatures as our property, simply because they do not have that faculty and are assumed to be of less consequence compared to us.

Yet in the Wisdom writings, Job orders Zophar to

> ask the beasts, and they will teach you,
>
> The birds of the air, and they will tell you;
>
> Or the plants of the earth, and they will teach you;
>
> And the fish of the sea will declare to you.
>
> Who among all these does not know that the hand of the Lord has done this?
>
> In his hand is the life of every living thing,
>
> And the breath (*ruach*) of all humankind. (Job 12:7)

For Locke, however, the Reason that links Men and God is, in Cartesian terms, a human "mental" faculty existing outside of space and time. The body, however, is an aggregate of atoms comprising a variety of material substances that follow the laws of physics. This categorization presupposes that reason or mind is immaterial, independent of the body's material substance. And that therefore bodies are forms of earthly property, like land, houses, or goods. In Locke's terms, our minds function as "divine" faculties, existing independently of time and space. Our bodies are, then, earthly, material property owned by our minds.

We may wish to vehemently reject this self-image. But to do so means rejecting the logic behind it that, by and large, still dominates Western self-perception. The principle on which Locke's logic rests is a systematic disentangling of our self-image from our image of Earth that he regards as not only possible but necessary and desirable. In a very real sense, holding and acting on such a principle results in a tendency to disdain our own earthiness. It also functions as an apparently cogent argument for rejecting its implications. This rejection in turn allows us to have a self-image that, as owners of the faculty of human reason, apparently entitles us to ownership of Earth. The basis for this is an image of immaterial Reason, or Mind, or Soul, as a divine faculty given only to human beings—or, as we shall see, to some of them.

Use the term "soul" and an unequivocal claim to this faculty, and its nature, emerges in a question from a Christian catechism:

Q. In what is man like to God?

A. Man is like to God in his soul.

This notional *dis*entangling of our self-image from that of Earth requires us to discriminate mentally (since we cannot do it physically) between the material, substantial, earthiness of our bodies and our "immaterial," self-sufficient, insubstantial, and (possibly) immortal or divine minds. These distinctions may be only implicit and more secular in our day compared with that of Locke, but they remain nonetheless powerful for being hidden. His mental analyses of our human selves belong within the traditional imagery employed by Plato, Christian teachers, and Descartes that is habitual in western educated cultures and has re-emerged in the Anthropic Principle. Its inevitable effect, then and now, was well understood by Locke's uneducated contemporary, the potter, when he discerned its implicit "disdain" for Earth.

Today we continue to show it, quite simply, in how we live. "Scaled up" from earth or land as property to the bodies of animals or women or both, the expressed legal and practical logic of mind over matter, of reason over feelings as the basis for human ownership of land, its creatures and its products has led to their exploitation and devastation on a global scale. Following on from European colonization, the rise and spread of global industrialization driven by unbridled greed for monetary profit has given an almost unstoppable momentum to claiming, buying, and selling land, animals, and raw materials and by doing so, enslaving indigenous peoples. This enslavement was originally justified, when deemed necessary, on the grounds that their bodies and lifestyles were more closely attached to, and related to earth. Or as we shall see, in the case of the Native Americans, that they left the land "vacant" that is, "unenclosed" or "undeveloped" by human labor. Now this exploitation is done in the service of "the market" and its "futures."

The colonial mindset that led eventually to the globalization of land as property remains all too evident even as the supply of land itself is running out. Its continuance relies on the added factor pointed out by Locke in his advice to American colonists: the use of a "small gold piece" that "altered the intrinsick value of things" useful to the life of Men. This "alteration" has meant that money was and continues to be used as a substitute for the land, its workforce or its produce.[9] In today's global markets even its materiality has been lost with the discontinuance of the gold standard. Now its putative monetary value as a bargaining counter relates to the "future" value of other material substances that, whether animal, vegetable, or mineral, are "owned"

9. Kurland and Lerner, *The Founders' Constitution.*

in advance, that is, bartered, gambled on, and exploited for profit in cyber-space. This is a realm from which any bodily, material presence appears totally excluded—unless we remind ourselves that it is controlled by human minds and fingers. And rather more dangerously, by human covetousness.

So far I have explored Locke's philosophical arguments to justify control of the material world by the human mind and its consequent exploitation of Earth. These do not, however, stand alone. As we have seen, in Locke's case they rested firmly on religious arguments based on seventeenth-century ver-sions and interpretations of the Bible. Such arguments still play a major role in perceptions of our earthiness or, more precisely, in some biblically-based religious interpretations of it today. So the Christian background to the pot-ter's remark will be the starting point for a discussion in the following chapters that will eventually take us back further still, to pre-Christian philosophies and even pre-literate European cultures. Yet however far back in human his-tory we look, the contemporary landscape provides mounting evidence for our earthiness and at the same time, our continuing, if not growing disregard for it and its fundamental life resources. The latest pointer (in the Fall of 2012) is Canada's decision to withdraw from the Kyoto climate change protocol on reducing carbon emissions.

When James Lovelock revived the name of Hesiod's Earth Goddess, Gaia, for a scientific theory embracing the Earth as a whole, merging its evolution and the evolution of life upon it (including our own) into a single process, not surprisingly it was met with some disdain. Decades later however, this percep-tion of Earth is routinely used as a basis for discussion not only scientifically but in society generally. For it is increasingly impossible for us to disentangle the effects of our self-understanding from the global implications of appar-ently random events. An evolutionary biologist (and later collaborator with Lovelock), the late Lynn Margulis, contributed to that understanding when she developed the theory of symbiogenesis: the long-term coming together of species leading to new forms of life. (Echoes here of Descartes's rebuttal of Kepler's homocentrism.) She centered attention on the emergence of life on this planet and how it became differentiated into what she calls its five kingdoms: bacteria, protoctista, fungi, plants, and animals. They belong, in different ways, to a whole Earth system that links life, all life, within the physi-cal realm. We humans, despite appearances and protestations to the contrary, are still very much part of that realm.[10] Quite simply, we do not and cannot exist outside it. These theories and the research on which they are based leave us in no doubt about our earthiness.

10. Margulis and Sagan, *What Is Life?*, 10.

Both Lovelock and Margulis have had the courage to stick with their research findings and give us contemporary categories for a more informed and accurate self-image that, by putting us firmly in our place within Gaia, lead us to appreciate and reverence her. For, as Margulis pointed out, we disdain her at our peril:

> Gaia is a tough bitch—a system that has worked for over three billion years without people. This planet's surface and its atmosphere and environment will continue to evolve long after people and prejudice are gone.[11]

Yet I think I am right in saying that there is nowhere on the planet's surface, or below or above that surface, that is not now claimed as the "property" of some nation, corporation, or individual, with all that that entails. Including a consistent prejudice against our "earthiness" in favor of human "reason."

11. Brockman, *The Third Culture*, 140.

4

Reformed Earth

The landscape of late sixteenth and seventeenth century Britain was littered with mutilated remains of the repudiated pre-Reformation past . . . Such desecrated structures and void spaces were graphic symbols of the vociferous rejection of the localization of the holy that characterized early Protestant polemic.[1]

In the Introduction to her book, *The Reformation of the Landscape*, Alexandra Walsham quotes from a "spiritual reflection" on a scene in the mid-Devon countryside written by a seventeenth-century Protestant English bishop, Joseph Hall. Then as now, mid-Devon was a patchwork of fields, hedges, and thickets of trees, dotted with villages and market towns nestling in the dips of its rolling hills and clustered in green valleys running alongside meandering rivers and streams. The panorama he glimpsed, she says, inspired him to remember the power and benevolence of the God "who had created the world for the benefit of the human beings."[2] Yet, as is clear from her account of how that bishop came to enjoy that landscape, this peaceful scene and his reflections on it followed the desecration of the pre-Reformation landscape and its religious structures. Their mutilated remains symbolized a rejection of the localization of the holy: of the material world as an embodiment of the divine.

1. Walsham, *The Reformation of the Landscape*, 233.
2. Ibid., 1.

It is impossible to do justice here to her nuanced and learned accounts of the religious and political struggles that characterized the transition from one era to another. On the eve of the Reformation, she writes, the landscape was covered with many overlapping membranes of religious memory and meaning: prehistoric earthworks and massive stone monuments bore mysterious witness to the forms of pagan religion practiced by its ancient and early medieval inhabitants. The arrival and entrenchment of Christianity overlaid these structures and natural topographical features (such as wells) with new religious associations. Heathen veneration of nature was gradually supplanted by reverence for God and his hierarchy. The miracles and pilgrims this attracted reflected a deep-seated belief that supernatural power was concentrated at particular geographical locations.[3]

But by the late sixteenth century, the landscape of Britain and Ireland was littered with the desecrated ruins of this era. They were part of the all-consuming crusade against idolatry that marked Calvinism in its first and later generations. In the eyes of a radical minority steeped in selected passages from the Hebrew scriptures, the landscape itself came to be seen as an arena filled with dangers to the souls of the faithful. And while changing theological priorities fostered a reevaluation of mediaeval sacred places, overall their sacredness was replaced (as in the bishop's reflections on the Devon countryside) by the mental category or doctrine of a desacralized Earth: one created by God for the benefit of human beings. In other words, as human property.

This takes us back to Locke. With the Restoration of the monarchy in 1660, the question of a possible religious patriarchal origin for political power became acute. It was in this situation, Laslett says, and against the background of his own Puritan beliefs, that Locke's *Treatises* and their doctrines took shape.[4] The word "doctrines" is apt. In *The First Treatise* these were shaped by Locke's close readings of both Hebrew and Septuagint versions of Genesis. He used these readings to argue against the image of monarchical power advocated by Royalist Sir Robert Filmer, expounding instead what he called *Adam's Title to Sovereignty by Donation*. Having established this model to his satisfaction, he went on to argue that God gave us *Dominion*, but not *Monarchical Power*, over all the *Irrational Animals of the World*.

There is an important resonance here with Paulinus's Roman Christian ministerial theory of landed power with its presupposition that the landowners' wealth lay in the hands of a single, all-powerful God to whom they were accountable for its use. From this point of view, Brown notes, nature was stripped of its ancient mystique of abundance and it was the will of God

3. Ibid., 80.
4. Laslett, *Locke*, 33–35.

alone—and not the semi-divine energy of nature—that caused the harvests to flourish every year. In the mosaics of the period no product of the wild or of the cultivated land was shown in its own right but presented as if it existed only to be "offered up" to the *dominus*, the owner of the estate—"preferably by ranks of neatly dressed and deferential peasants."[5]

Locke's Puritan antipathy to Filmer's advocacy of monarchical power is evident in the assertion that

> Whatever God gave by the words of this Grant (Genesis 1:28), it was not to Adam in particular, exclusive of all other men; whatever Dominion he had thereby, it was not a Private Dominion, but a dominion in common with the rest of Mankind.[6]

Locke backed up this egalitarian argument—which gives sovereignty to Adam as representative of mankind—by ridiculing the notion that Adam was made *sole Proprietor* of the whole of Earth's resources:

> Or how will the Possession even of the whole Earth give any one a Sovereign Arbitrary Authority over the Persons of Men? The most specious thing to be said is, that he that is Proprietor of the whole World, may deny all the rest of Mankind Food, and so at his pleasure starve them, if they will not acknowledge his Sovereignty and Obey his Will.[7]

Indeed, Locke argues, it is more reasonable to think that God who bid mankind increase and multiply should give all persons a right to make use of food, clothing and the other conveniences of life, the materials for which God had provided so abundantly. He was ahead of his time in arguing *against* the notion of sovereignty within the family on the grounds that God gave dominion to both Adam and Eve when he said:

> Let us make Man in our Image, after our likeness, and let Them have dominion over the fish of the sea, and over the birds of the air, and over the cattle, and over all the earth, and over every creeping thing that creeps upon the earth (Genesis 1:26).[8]

And finally, looking forward to *The Second Treatise*, he argued *for* the notion that

---

5. Brown, *Through the Eye of a Needle*, 238f.

6. Laslett, *Locke*, 161.

7. Ibid., 169.

8. See ibid., 161–62.

> Property, whose Original is from the Right a Man has to use any of
> the inferior Creatures, for the Subsistence and Comfort of his life,
> is for the benefit and sole Advantage of the Proprietor, so that he
> may even destroy the thing that he has property in by his use of it,
> where need requires.[9]

There is material enough in these quotations for lengthy discussion and contemporary formulations both for and against Locke's arguments against "sovereignty" as a mode of human government. My main interest here is the meaning he attaches to "Possession of the whole Earth," reiterated in the *Second Treatise*. For him, it means that men have the power of life and death over all "irrational," "inferior," or, in today's less demeaning term, "other-than-human" creatures. The right of men to possess the land on which they live is taken for granted. It is also important to note that in seventeenth-century England, Locke could appeal to and rely on the authority and language of the vernacular King James Bible to establish and support his claim to Man's "possession" of such power as being part of his proprietorship of the "whole" Earth.

Support for such a claim was then a major formative influence in British politics and, as we saw in the American *Founders' Constitution*, in their colonial policies also. Nowadays, while the biblical authority for it may seldom if ever be publicly or politically invoked, it serves, in practice, as social and cultural justification of what is taken to be tacitly agreed and thereby unassailable. Including its legitimizing and legalizing of the routine destruction of living creatures when classed as human "property."

This Reformation legacy reflected the fundamental ambivalence of Protestant attitudes toward previous categorizing of the universe as God's work and was enhanced by the impact of early modern advances in science. We saw this already in the disagreement between Kepler and Descartes as to whether or not "all things have been made [by God] for man." Later, Thomas Hardy's *Country Songs* gave an ecologically humble answer to this implicit question that reflected the Cartesian rather than the Lockean vision and reflects the stance of most earth scientists today:

> Let me enjoy the earth no less
> Because the all-enacting Might
> That fashioned forth its loveliness
> Had other aims than my delight.[10]

9. Ibid., 209.
10. Thomas Hardy, "Let Me Enjoy."

Or, it must be added, other aims than enriching those with the power to appropriate it and "legitimately" destroy earth's creatures. Walsham remarks that when early modern Protestants pondered the origins of their world, they intuitively turned (as Locke did) to the book of Genesis for guidance. That entailed an immediate "re-forming" of a previous cultural understanding of the landscape and our relationship with it. Historically, she identifies that with a Roman Catholic attitude, expressed in and based largely on religious rituals accessible to all believers, literate and illiterate alike. Rather than a Puritan strict adherence to written scripture, *"God's Great Book."*

The clash between the two approaches and their ambivalent relationship had lasting consequences. They included

> repeated episodes of iconoclastic violence designed to purge the landscape of lingering reminders of the Catholic and pagan past and to demonstrate that sacred power did not reside in physical objects, structures or places.[11]

In short, the realities of political power struggles led to humans claiming sovereignty and ownership over land that shattered those mental categories that assigned that ownership ultimately to divine power: manifest in certain physical structures, objects, or places. Relationship between the material and the spiritual, and our access through the former to the latter, was instead defined by their difference from each other. This was an open denigration of the earthly landscape. Its intrinsic sacralization was dealt a devastating and all too visible blow that denied the immanence of the holy by separating it from natural features. One such, St. Winefride's Well in North Wales, still bears significant traces of pilgrimages to its healing waters. At Lough Derg in Ireland, pilgrimages have never ceased.

In Locke's case, the defining difference between divine indwelling and human property was found in the biblical description of God's "grant" of Earth to men. But that depended, and still depends on what was and is read into that description and how it was and may be interpreted. The Genesis text says unequivocally that God saw that everything created, that is, everything on earth, in the waters and in the heavens, "was good" (Gen 1:31). And in regard to our relationship with earth, a recent translation of the Hebrew text gives God's final command to Adam and Eve as: "Serve the ground from which you were taken."[12] However translated, God did not say: "Use it as your property" or "Destroy its creatures."

These injunctions ascribed to God by Locke ensured that

11. Walsham, *The Reformation of the Landscape*, 327.
12. Genesis 3:23 translated by Korsak, *At the Start*, 11.

> the corrosive distrust of the immanence of the holy that under-
> pinned these successive phases of godly reformation coexisted
> with the notion that the natural environment was alive with moral,
> supernatural and spiritual significance. . . . [T]he longstanding as-
> sumption that the landscape bore witness to the activities of God
> as its initial Creator and eternal curator, and to His plan for its
> human inhabitants described in the pages of Scripture were in-
> herited tenets tested by developments that constantly redefined
> the frontiers between nature and supernature and questioned the
> precise mechanisms by which Providence worked.[13]

The corrosive distrust of the immanence of the holy was physically manifested
in brutal clashes with those who held opposing notions or indeed quite different notions. As we shall see, these clashes played an integral role in colonial
conquests. If challenged, they were supported by appealing not only to the
pre-eminent guiding role of scripture but also to differing interpretations of
scripture. The ambivalence of the texts themselves, especially in regard to humanity's relationship to God and to earth and in regard to God's relationship
to all earth's creatures guaranteed the victory of the strongest.[14] It meant that
when "scripture" as a literary source of access to God was mediated through
a culturally dominant, educated male Christian elite of Protestant clerics and
pious statesmen like Locke, it could be used to curb what was seen as the
perennial tendency of people to transform visible things into idols: in short,
to venerate the effects of Creation rather than their (presumed) divine, immaterial author and creator. The practice attributed to Locke's contemporary,
Oliver Cromwell, of stabling his soldiers' horses in the sanctuaries of churches
once Catholic, symbolized the violent rejection of such a tendency.

Then and now the presumed duality of material/immaterial was and
still is invoked by Christian churches to consistently downgrade the material.
Access to the divine was presumed to be and to a large extent still is seen as
guarded and guaranteed only by obedience to clergy and their teachings. That
has left less educated classes no religious voice to challenge those teachings
and particularly their effects on the lives of the illiterate poor. In these circumstances, as Calvin asserted, the sacred word of scripture has remained a mode
of communication in which the deification of nature, rather than the glorifica-
tion of its Maker, is seen as a danger of which all Christians should be aware.

Calvin saw the end results of Creation as a product of divine work and
wisdom, "a most beautiful theatre" and "a large and splendid mansion gor-
geously constructed and exquisitely furnished." Here people could see "the

13. Walsham, *The Reformation of the Landscape*, 327.

14. Primavesi, *From Apocalypse to Genesis*, 203–4.

immense treasures of wisdom and goodness exhibited in the creatures, as in so many mirrors."[15] A century later, Locke viewed those same creatures as "irrational" and "inferior" compared to us. But however differently viewed, Reformed clergy and laypeople remained convinced that the nature of the physical world was an important *unwritten* supplement to the canonical books that the patriarchs, prophets, Gospel writers, and apostles "had inscribed on parchment in ages past."

How you viewed that supplement depended on the expertise of those who could read the written text. Indeed they rhapsodized about the iconography of nature—but on the understanding that the physical world was to be read as a way of instructing humanity about its Maker and his divine sovereignty. John Maynard urged his readers to

> spend more hours in studying this great Booke of Nature, which the Lord hath spread open before us, therein describing unto us those invisible things of his Eternal Power and God-head in such plain and legible Characters, that he which runneth may read them; every main part being (as it were) a several Volume, the Heaven, the Aire, the Earth and Waters, every Creature in these being a several leaf or Page; every part of each a Creature; every natural property, quality or created virtue in each being a several line, or (at least), word or syllable.[16]

By discerning these "invisible things" of God's Eternal Power in the great Booke of Nature, Protestants believed that they were taking their cue from Paul in the New Testament:

> For the invisible things of him from the creation of the world are clearly seen being understood by the things that are made; even his eternal power (Rom 1:20; King James version).

They glimpsed God at work in this visible world of infinite mystery; an incorporeal being who was, by definition, sublime and inscrutable. "What is this worlde," asked Calvin, glossing the paradox at the heart of this key New Testament passage, "but a lively image . . . in the which God sheweth and declareth himself. For albeit he be invisible in his essence, yet sheweth he himself by his workes, to the ende we should worship him." In Locke's lifetime, London pastor George Walker insisted that it was through his exterior operations that

15. Walsham, *The Reformation of the Landscape*, 331.
16. Ibid., 330.

Christians were able "as in a glass [to] behold the glory of God with open face (the vaile of ignorance being removed)."[17]

But Locke, as we have seen, did not engage with this paradox in which visible/invisible signifies human mental categorization and not an inherent, divinely ordered separation. Treating them as separate did, of course, make his message more accessible and acceptable because unequivocally one-sided. Rather than serving the Earth from which we are taken or foregrounding the mystery of divine presence within all Creation, he focused on the human faculty of Reason as the differentiating factor between ourselves and all other earthly creatures. Using it to make distinctions between them and us was what was "reasonable" for him. In this, he could be seen to follow Augustine, who himself followed Platonic philosophy in maintaining that the bodily senses that reported information about the material world themselves belonged to the material realm and therefore should not be trusted. Only the human intellect, the *rational constituent of the soul of man,* created by God and *placed above the material realm,* could arrive at true knowledge.[18]

But Augustine also argued that because we are made in the image of God, we can receive this knowledge directly from God by means of a revelation *within* Creation, that is, within the "material" realm. As, however, most people are incapable of discovering the truth themselves, Augustine, like Locke, held that God had instituted the scriptures to help them. The text of scripture is, he emphasized, the most trustworthy witness for the truth of God. But in his *Epistulae,* he insisted that the created world itself, the greatest of all visible things, testifies to the truth of scripture: "The earth is our big book; in it I read as fulfilled what I read as promised in the book of God."[19]

The important point here is that for Augustine, while literacy and reason were implicit in the study of the Bible text, they represented both the way to knowledge and the starting point for the process of reasoning. The study of the visible world, of God's creation and manifestation, was an equally valid way to acquire knowledge about its Creator. Following Augustine, in the ninth century Johannes Scottus Eriugena remarked: "For even Abraham knew God not through the letters of Scripture which had not yet been composed, but by the revolutions of the stars."[20]

This insight into the biblical text itself as witness to a knowledge of God outside of and preceding that text, and therefore open to illiterate and literate alike, is a stunning rebuttal of any insistence on that knowledge being

17. Ibid., 328–34.

18. See Lozovsky, *The Earth Is Our Book,* 142–43.

19. Ibid., 142.

20. Ibid., 142–43.

accessible only to the learned and literate. In Locke's particular historical and religious milieu, categorizing the very nature and status of Earth on the basis of biblical knowledge of God was deeply embedded in the culture. But in his case, the focus was on *self-knowledge*: on biblical images of ourselves in relation to Earth.

This conjunction of self-image and Earth image supported, and still supports, a human self-image in which our possession of Reason or Rationality is taken as evidence of our superiority over all other creatures. Or more precisely, the rationality of some of us in relation to others and in relation to Earth and all other-than-human creatures. This self-image, as we shall see, played a major role in attitudes to the indigenous inhabitants of colonized lands, both human and other-than-human. In Locke's day, it formed part of the self-understanding of a literate elite that allowed them to set cultural norms by appealing to scriptural norms. In other words, to norms culturally identified and interpreted by them.

At the same time, by virtue of their literary access to the biblical sources of those norms, they exercised quasi-divine authority over the views of Earth held by the majority of the population. This resulted implicitly and explicitly, in every sense and in every way, in the elevation of the intellect or mind over the bodily senses. With few enough exceptions for them to be discounted, this quasi-divine authority was exercised by men alone. And this sex discrimination (as it is named today) ensured that women were almost wholly categorized by their ability to give birth to new life, fulfilling a role analogous to that of earth. Man remained, in Locke's words, the "Principal and Nobler Agent in Generation." That in turn helped to identify women as more "earthy" than men and so relegated them to the subordinate role of generating and fostering new life.

So wherever Scripture was key to describing human relationships, interpretations of women's "earthiness" and their consequent subordination were based on certain readings of Genesis. In these, Eve's "tempting" Adam to disobedience was interpreted as sin and linked to their being excluded from a paradisal relationship with Earth and its creatures. From then on their lives, or rather the lives of those who were not "proprietors" of Earth as holders of "property," were seen as rightly subject to toil in order to counteract the barrenness of the soil. And as subject to enmity between them and all other-than-human creatures.

This biblically-based history of human earthiness, in which our relationships with the natural world are taken to be compromised almost from the beginning, reinforced rather than contradicted one in which the temptation to idolatry was associated with things made from earthly matter—such as the potter's hand-warmer. It meant that they were to be disdained in favor of the immaterial and the divine—as revealed to human Reason. As the opposite of these "godly" goods, earthly things were associated with ungodly pagan practices. Yet at the same time it was held that God infused living things with motion, effected their mutations and alterations and checked and bridled the elements by his eternal counsels.[21]

Locke's arguments for the overarching role of God in regard to our ownership and control of Earth's creatures, its resources and their use, were based on reason interpreting revelation:

> Whether we consider natural Reason, which tells us that Men, once born, have a right to their Preservation, and consequently to Meat and Drink, and such other things as Nature affords for their Subsistence. Or Revelation, which gives us an account of those Grants God made of the World to Adam, and to Noah, and his Sons 'tis very clear that God, as King David says, Psalm CXV, xvi, has given the Earth to the Children of Men, given it to Mankind in common.[22]

These disembodied human categories, Reason and Revelation, were taken as guides to the pattern of events; as immaterial mechanisms that determined whether, for instance, the waters would cover the dry places of the earth and prevent life from flourishing. The order of nature was seen to be fragile and precarious, lacking any inherent capacity to look after or sustain itself. The visible world was seen as a testament to the perpetual intervention of the Almighty in the cosmos he had created from nothing. Within it, men, and only men, and of them only learned men, were able to receive and interpret puzzling phenomena or incidents whose natural explanations were hidden from the majority of the populace.

It was this elevation of reason and revelation above an earthiness shared with all living beings that the potter discerned as an implicit "disdain" of Earth. Today, that refusal is commonly expressed by regarding and describing "earth" as "dirt," "soil" or even "filth." Now, thanks to advances in science, being "dirtied," "soiled," or made "filthy" is synonymous with a bacterial threat to our well-being. Associating human flesh with earth does not convey an acceptable self-image. Socially, being "earthy" carries an impression of being ill-educated and uncouth while being "dirty" is totally unacceptable: we recoil from it as a sign of poverty, laziness, or potentially deadly infection. It is assumed to be based on a lack of education or, at best, on misfortune in not having enough

21. Walsham, *The Reformation of the Landscape*, 335.
22. Kurland and Lerner, *The Founders' Constitution*, 1.

money to keep the body "clean and healthy." Therefore, not worthy of respect but of disdain.

While we are distanced historically from the potter's milieu, this attitude to earth persists, and remains an important and influential cultural link between our lives and his. This struck me forcibly when I attended a burial according to the ritual taken from *The Book of Common Prayer*. A product of the early days of the English Reformation, it was first published in 1549, in the reign of Edward VI. It was reintroduced in a reformed version by Elizabeth I in 1552, and in 1604 James I ordered some further changes. In 1662, following the events leading up to and including the Civil War, there was another major revision that remains the official prayer book of the Church of England.

With some local variations, it is used today in churches inside and outside the Anglican Communion in over 50 different countries and has been translated into 150 different languages. Other Protestant denominations have borrowed from it, so that its marriage and burial rituals have found their way into those of other denominations. As Diarmaid MacCulloch remarks, the Prayer Book is by no means an historical document; its presence or its memory is the main thing that unites the not especially united family of churches that now calls itself the Anglican Communion.[23]

In these times of global mass media, the images of earth and of ourselves portrayed in these rituals have a reach far beyond the members of Christian denominations actively participating in them. In the case of major figures, burials in particular are now attended by, listened to, or televised worldwide and then seen and heard in far larger numbers than those attending other church services. The graveside setting gives the ceremonial language an emotional impact beyond what is said. There is an acute sense of kinship between the dead, the living, and the place on earth they inhabit at that particular moment that gives an imaginative potency to the words used. This is accentuated by the setting, by the clergy's ceremonial robes and, in some cases, by solemn and emotive music.

What did I hear proclaimed about the human body's relationship with Earth when the cortege moved to the graveside for the prayer of committal? As relatives and friends of the deceased were invited to throw flowers or earth onto the coffin the priest said:

> [W]e therefore commit her body to the ground; earth to earth, ashes to ashes, dust to dust; in sure and certain hope of the resurrection to eternal life through our Lord Jesus Christ; who shall change *our vile body* (Philippians 3:21) that it may be like his glorious body. [Italics added]

23. MacCulloch, "Mumpsimus, Sumpsimus," 15.

At this solemn and memorable moment, being "*earthy*" is presented as being "*vile*": with the promise of that being changed *after death* into all that is "*unearthly*" or "*eternal,*" that is, incorrupt, glorious, and divine. Who would not thereby feel entitled to disdain our earthiness? What preacher explains that the distinctions made in the Pauline paradox express the coexistence—not the separation—of what we call "glory" and "vileness," "spirit" and "body," "life" and "death," "corrupt" and "incorrupt"?

In his book *Dirt: The Ecstatic Skin of Earth,* William Bryant Logan observes how that coexistence continually reforms earth into living bodies:

> But the soil is all of the Earth that is really ours. The seasons, with their heat and their cold, make the soil. The storms make the soil, with water, the most powerful substance on Earth. The winds make the soil, spreading dust across thousands of miles. The tides make the soil, stirring the river deltas and their fertile slimes. And above all, the trees and the plants, the dead and the digested, the eaters and the eaten, make the soil. . . . Soil appears where life does, and its characteristic is to build where erosion destroys. . . . Everywhere, creatures and minerals together make their characteristic soils.[24]

Logan describes his insight as using our eyes to conceive the "livingness" of the soil. In other words, using our bodily senses *and* reason to realize that earthiness (*humus*) is the "ground" of our being "human."

24. Logan, *Dirt,* 96–97.

5

Classical Earth

*The continuing partnership between orality and literacy, ear and eye,
required Plato, writing in the crucial moment of transition from one to
the other, to reassert the primacy of speaking and hearing in personal oral
response, even as he wrote. . . . But it was the written which had made his
own profession possible, and his literary output—the first extensive and
coherent body of written speculative thought in the history of mankind—
testifies as much.*[1]

The previous chapter examined the textual bases of a prevailing self-image
that distinguishes "us" from our earthly bodies on the grounds of our having
a soul or intellect. In this chapter I will go back to an earlier historic clash
in self-perception when the primacy of speaking and hearing prevailed and
with it, a quite different view of ourselves, Earth, and the divine. Then, a European understanding of our species' place and role in the world was largely
shared through oral transmission: that is, in performance based on memory.
Accumulated knowledge about Earth's history and our own was retained and
recited in the form of myths, plays, poems, ritual, and song. These were all-
important channels of communication in a culture where oral repetition was a
major factor in creating and sustaining a shared self-image. It shaped societies

1. Havelock, *The Muse Learns to Write*, 111–12.

psychologically and socially, and played an essential role in maintaining continuity of culture.

Hesiod, for example, speaks eloquently of the farmer's hopes and fears, and reinforces his own warnings about the future by giving his audience three contradictory pictures of the harvest: one of the good harvest that comes if we follow his advice, one of the bad harvest that comes if we ignore it, and finally, one of a harvest rescued from disaster—at the last moment—through the inscrutable will of Zeus. The vivid detail of his descriptions manipulates our feelings of identification. First, we share the reasonable and cheerful expectations of the early plowman, only to be crushed—in the second description—by the dismal prospects haunting the mind of the farmer and, as we experience his despair, we also feel, with the gradual dawning prospect of a remedy, a sudden hope.[2]

This oral tradition and transmission of learning, based largely on the works of Hesiod, Homer, and Euripides, was the backdrop to Plato's explicit rejection of "poetry" as a proper resource for higher education. It is impossible to understand this rejection unless we come to terms with what Eric Havelock calls that most baffling of all words in his philosophic vocabulary, the Greek term *mimesis*. In *The Republic* Plato first employs it as a stylistic classification defining dramatic as opposed to descriptive composition. In other words, as a technique of verbal communication. As one reads on, however, it becomes quite clear that he is profoundly hostile to the range and versatility of expression that dramatization makes possible. Why so? The reason lies with its possible effects on "the young guardians of his state," particularly the kind of bodily "identification" with the farmer evoked by Hesiod. For Plato's pupils are to become the citizen-soldiers whose assigned tasks will require a different sort of character and ethical judgment. So Plato shifts the context of the argument against *mimesis* from the artistic to the educational sphere.

For him, nothing less than the moral condition of the pupil-guardian is at stake. This, for him, is nurtured through the correct kind of "imitation" which does not, in his opinion, follow from a continual engagement in reciting or performing poetry. For poetry indulges in constant illusionism, confusion, and irrationality. It "cripples the intellect of the listeners" and is a "shadow-show of phantoms, like those images seen in the darkness on the wall of the cave." In direct contrast to this, Platonic reality is rational, scientific and logical, or it is nothing.[3]

It is difficult for us today to see poetry as a danger to morals. That, in itself, signals a victory for Plato. So what, precisely, was he reacting against?

2. Nelson, *God and the Land*, 55.
3. Havelock, *The Muse Learns to Write*, 20–25, 38.

In his authoritative study, *Mimesis: The Representation of Reality in Western Literature*, Eric Auerbach offers insights into Homer's dramatic style that give *mimesis* a larger cultural background and focus than that of Plato's city state. He defines the mimetic style as one that caters to the need for externalization of phenomena in terms perceptible to the senses—rather than being directed at their supposed opposites: reason and logic.

The example he chooses, from Homer's *Odyssey*, centers our attention and that of the audience on Odysseus's visible and palpable bodily scar. The result of a juvenile encounter with a boar, whenever it is exhibited or referred to in relation to other persons and later events, it brings and keeps those persons and events together in the listeners' minds. Boundaries in time and space are clearly delimited; those before the scar, those beside it, and those after it are linked to other complexes of events that do not depend on it but can be conceived in relation to it without difficulty. This didactic function was precisely what Plato rejected in the oral tradition; seeing it as "a kind of versified encyclopedia" in which effective memorization depended on the use of vision supported by rhythmic sound.

But for Homer's audience, says Auerbach, the procession of externalized, visible and palpable phenomena before them allows them to move back and forth from scene to scene and, at the same time, brings their own relationships together so that nothing is fragmentary or half-illuminated. Delight in physical existence is everything, and the epic's highest aim is to make that delight perceptible to us. It bewitches and ingratiates itself with us as we live with the reality of the lives depicted there—as was also the case with Hesiod's farmer. While we read the poems, then or now, it does not matter whether or not we believe them to be true. This "real" world into which we are lured exists for itself. It contains nothing but itself. The Homeric poems contain no teaching and no second meaning. Homer can be analyzed, but he cannot be interpreted. Attempts to do so are forced and foreign.[4]

Some scholars may argue with Auerbach's conclusion. But it explains to some extent Plato's rejection of poetry as "crippling the intellect." At the same time it also obscures the enormity of the task involved: nothing less than the rejection of at least one thousand years of oral and written cultural ascendancy. At first transmitted by memory, the earliest written versions of Homer's scattered songs date back to around 280 BCE. These were compiled from bits on earlier papyri as well as from citations by earlier authors that had been circulating for at least three centuries. The oral composition of the *Iliad* may have started around 1500 BCE. Its longevity stems from the content: a

4. Auerbach, *Mimesis*, 6–7, 13, 16.

powerful affirmation of the warrior's creed at a time when all able-bodied free men were called to arms in a Greece of independent city states.

Its memorable use of detail in recounting events still resonates through the written text:

> The greaves first he set about his legs . . . next he put on about his chest the corselet . . . and about his shoulders he flung his sword . . . and he took up his richly inlaid, valorous shield. . . .
> Spears cut through temples, foreheads, navels, chests; joyful victors strip their victims of their armour and gain extra delight from imagining their weeping mothers and wives.[5]

Plato's written texts were, however, quite different in character and style. They formulated a new conceptual type of language and thought which, over time, has helped to replace that fostered and fed by oral narrative with its externalized, sensual, vocalized thinking. The change from this to internalized reactions and thought processes produced a psychological, indeed physiological shift in the ratio of the senses used to discover and enact a common self-perception. The bodily shift—from sound to sight, from ear to eye, from watching and listening to reading the written word—was fundamental in redirecting the development of European culture. We seem now to have reached its apogee in the visual "memory" of the search engines we use on the Internet.

But that is just the external evidence of a physiological and psychological shift begun by Plato. His advocacy of the didactic function of written words led to formulations of new concepts and abstract ways of thinking about ourselves—and about how we think—that were and would remain visibly accessible to literate cultures, or rather, to those who are culturally literate. Physical bodily performance, on the other hand—however skilled or creative—gradually lost its key role as a method of instruction. Now its sensually loaded character generally serves only to enhance or perpetuate a particular recognizable self-understanding.

Platonic "formulations of new concepts and abstract ways of thinking about ourselves and about how we think" is an extended definition of what Teilhard de Chardin called "mental categorizing." A visible difference between this type of language and thought and sensually loaded, externalized "sound" thinking has indeed produced a psychological, even physiological shift in Western cultural norms. The difference is displayed on this page in the formal distance and distinctions between written words that denote the physical difference between an "invisible" traceless orality and the continued presence, effectiveness, and impact of visible and precisely punctuated

5. Luttwak, "The *Iliad* by Homer," 3–8.

literature. It connotes, consciously and subconsciously, a separation between words, thoughts, and thinker that can be measured both visually and in time; staying with or lingering over some or moving rapidly on to others. There is no human intermediary between us and the written record of an invisible author's experiences, feelings, opinions, and thoughts. Thinking has become a largely solitary occupation.

So as Mary Midgley points out, it is now through the thinker's wider perspective, more comprehensive viewpoint and longer view backwards and forwards in life that more thoughtful individuals still see the continuous course of their own conduct and can compare it with that of others.[6] As indeed is happening here. But how far has this lack of a more comprehensive, other-inclusive viewpoint distanced us from an active, working perception of our belonging within the living, fragile community of life once typified by Odysseus's scarred body? How deeply moved are we by daily scenes of carnage displayed worldwide on screens large and small? How identified are we with farmers' anxieties about the prospect of a good harvest? Or how influenced are we by documentaries detailing the extinction of species? How does such televisual presentation, available or dismissed by pressing a control button, affect or foster our ability to engage with our history of shared earthiness?

In pre-literate times, that wider perspective was based on a "whole-body" awareness of the past as still present in human communities, their joys, sorrows, struggles, and environments; and on our ability to continuously receive, communicate, and store information about it in our personal and collective bodily memory. Once that ability was or is neglected or lost, it becomes increasingly difficult to recall or repeat what we have heard—or read. These qualitative, bodily differences between our interactions with and responses to sound, sight, touch, and smell mean that with the cultural ascendancy of written or other visual methods of storing knowledge, the reading eye of the solitary self has come to supplant a whole-body experience as the chief organ used to share and retain what we know about ourselves, our historic past, and our earthy origins. That knowledge is no longer stored in bodily communal memory within a shared landscape but on library shelves or, increasingly, on the ethereal Internet.

This evolutionary change in access to knowledge has changed the body's role as a living intermediary between us and the physical world. Or more precisely, it has changed our perception of the role played by our bodies in that mediation. The "whole body" experience has been subsumed into the sensual response of the eye, replacing the complex interactions between thoughts, feelings, and memories still aroused by the personal voice of oral

6. Midgley, *The Solitary Self*, 58.

performance. There the listeners' response is one in which each individual plays an active role in the communal response to the actions and emotions performed, evoked, or recounted by the poet, speaker, singer, or dramatist—as still happens today at pop concerts.

But we would not find Plato at one of these! For it was occasions such as these that he precisely had in mind in his argument against "poetry": a catch-all label for recited, memorized, and potentially empathic knowledge. His ideal education was based primarily on his doctrine of the autonomous, lone individual identified as the seat of rational thought. Judgment on the actions and motives of others would then be a proper, considered response—rather than sympathetic identification with their situation. In other words, *mimesis* is wholly incompatible with objectified, rational knowledge:

> The imitative process of "making yourself like somebody else" is now disclosed with compelling force to be a "surrender" of one's self, a "following along" while we "identify" with the emotions of others. . . . To this pathology [sic] of identification Plato opposes the "polity in oneself," the "city of man's own soul," and affirms the absolute necessity of building an inner self-consistency. This becomes possible only if we reject the whole process of poetic identification. And this identification is pleasurable; it appeals to the unconscious instinct. It means surrender to a spell.[7]

Plato, says Havelock, affirms over and over again that the ideal of free autonomous reflection and cogitation is a necessary challenge to sense impressions. The self-governing personality comes to symbolize the power to think, to cogitate, to calculate, and to know; in distinction from the capacity to see, to hear, and to feel. Rodin's sculpture *The Thinker* epitomizes this total isolation—a body that (supposedly) sees, feels, and hears nothing. There is no discernible scar on it: it is close to being a device for thinking in terms of what (a) is purely abstract and (b) is situated in a timeless space which always "is" and never "is not." It is accepted as a generic representation of the human person, and taken for granted as such by all educated viewers of it today.

This cultural acceptance follows historically from Plato's insistence that his contemporaries must turn away from the panorama of sensual response and focus instead upon the abstracted object *per se* as the only worthwhile or even possible object of thought. He sometimes identifies this object as a Form and also speaks of the Forms (plural) as furnishing a methodology or intellectual discipline that is familiar to his readers. It has become usual to speak of this as Plato's Theory of Forms. Yet it is important to note, says Havelock,

7. Havelock, *Preface to Plato*, 206–7.

that he can use the term "form" over and over again without a capital letter to mean type or class or category. Capitalized, it denotes that which "is" and is "unseen": the integrity of the "itself *per se*," conceived as "category" or "principle" or "property." To understand the Platonic revolution we must begin with this language and not with the Forms. Or more accurately, just some of us. As Plato himself put it:

> For the majority of men it is impossible to entertain beauty itself instead of the many beautifuls, or any specific "itself" instead of the many specifics . . . so the majority can never be intellectuals.

The phrase "itself *per se*," the *Ding an Sich*, stresses the simple purity of the "object" gathered together in isolation from any contamination with anything else or any particular instance. "Dogness," for instance, as opposed to *that* dog jumping around over there. (My husband's example.) This, says Havelock, indicates a mental act that quite literally corresponds to the Latin term "abstraction." The "object" that the "subject" has to think about has been "abstracted from," that is, literally "torn out" of the epic context. Or, staying with the epic, we are to think about Odysseus's "scar" apart from his body. This offered a new frame of discourse and vocabulary to the European mind, one taken for granted today as the discourse of educated men. It seldom occurs to us that once upon a time it was necessary for it to have been discovered and defined and insisted on, so that we could easily and complacently inherit it.[8]

But again, only some of us. Stone, papyrus, metal, parchment, and paper record this progression toward the literacy of an elite whose ability to use abstract concepts such as "property," "soul," "government," "justice," and "reason" both implied and reinforced their social ascendancy. The process of abstracting Platonic Forms from earthy, animal, sensually empathetic bodily realities was so successful that its vocabulary became and remains more or less standard as these concepts and modes of thought were passed on from one educated generation to the next. So John Locke's "author-ity," as someone literate enough to compose and write *An Essay Concerning Human Understanding*, meant that this essay and his treatises on the concept of government remain standard reference works today. His authoritative use of that concept, itself based on written sources, retains its sway over our self-image, our image of Earth, and our perception of the relationship between the two. The appeal to scripture in his writings is also symptomatic of an enduring preference for written sources.

Locke's titles reflect the content of his writings. But in the history of the written word this has not always been the case. A part may become identified

8. Ibid., 4.

with the whole, creating an expectation that accords with the title but is belied by much of the substance of the text. This, says Havelock, applies with full force to Plato's treatise, the *Republic*, in which the disjuncture between title and content is most evident in the tenth and last book that opens with an examination of poetry, not politics. It places the poet in the same company as the painter, arguing that both produce a version of experience that is twice removed from reality. So their work is at best frivolous and at worst danger-ous. Therefore it must be excluded from the education system. For Plato, it is a kind of disease, a mental poison that requires an antidote. That antidote is a knowledge "of what things really are." He winds up his argument with this uncompromising statement:

> Crucial indeed is the struggle—more crucial than we think—the choice that makes us good or bad—to keep faithful to righteous-ness and virtue in the face of temptation, be it of fame or money or power, or of poetry—yes, even of poetry.

We may conclude, remarks Havelock, that as he exhorts us to fight the good fight against poetry (like a Greek Saint Paul warring against the powers of darkness), he has either lost all sense of proportion or that his target cannot be poetry as we understand it, but something more fundamental to and powerful in the ancient Greek experience. Plato attacks the very form and substance of the poetic statement, its images, its rhythms, and its choice of language. Nor is he less hostile to the range of experience that she (Poetry) makes available to us. For poetry can represent a thousand situations and portray a thousand emotions and, by doing so, unlock a corresponding fund of sympathetic re-sponses in us, that is, in our bodies. For Plato, this dramatic empathy is a kind of psychic poison, one to which we must always have an antidote ready. We need this protection against poetry and her dangers because, he says, "[W]e have our city of the soul (*psyche*) to protect against her."[9]

What is the soul to be protected from? From the "psychic poison" of sympathetic, bodily responses. The presupposition is that the soul is separate from and superior to the body. Locke spells out this Platonic distinction in the clearest possible terms when he compares the ideas we have of soul and body. They involve, he says, a comparison between the complex idea of an immate-rial spirit (soul) and our complex idea of a material body:

> Our idea of body, as I think of it, is an extended solid substance, capable of communicating motion by impulse; and our idea of our

9. Ibid., 5.

soul, as an immaterial spirit, is of a substance that thinks, and has
a power of exciting motion in the body, by will, or thought.[10]

This material distinction between body and soul is basic to Locke's idea of
"reason" which is, he says, a faculty that "distinguishes man from beasts and
wherein he much surpasses them." For reason is necessary for "the enlargement of our knowledge and regulating our assent." It does this by "ordering
the chain of ideas to discover what connection there is in each link of the
chain" so that the extremes are held together and so draw into view the truth
sought for.[11] For him, Plato's definition of the *psyche* means that the solid
earthy substance of our body is ruled by the immaterial spirit or soul; that is
what "thinks" and so has the power to move the body by will or by thought.

Using these mental categories allows us to infer that this "rule" of spirit
over body is necessary because the body is mortal: subject to physical gain and
loss; endowed with the faculty of sensation dependent on external stimulation
as well as with desire and its mixture of pain and pleasure, fear and anger:

> Mastery of these would lead to a good life: subjection to them to
> a wicked life. And anyone who lives well for his appointed time
> returns home to his native star. . . .
>
> Anyone who fails to do so will be reborn as a woman. And if
> he still does not refrain from wrong, be changed into some animal
> suitable to his particular kind of wrongdoing, with no respite from
> change and suffering.[12]

Locke's dualistic self-understanding depends on this radical change introduced by Plato into the meaning of the Greek word *psyche*. Instead of signify-
ing a man's ghost or wraith, or his breath or life-blood, a thing devoid of sense
and self-consciousness, it came to mean "the ghost that thinks"; one that is
capable both of moral decision and scientific cognition. It is the seat of moral
responsibility, something infinitely precious with an immortal essence unique
in the whole realm of Nature.

These claims about what it means to be human, with categorical distinctions between a mortal body and an immortal soul being used to implicitly
devalue the former and enhance the value of the latter, are more usually associated with Christian religious structures and strictures than with philosophy.
Which is scarcely surprising since it was through hierarchical educational
institutions that they were assimilated into European teaching and have affected cultural perceptions of our humanity. Their underlying assumption of

10. Locke, *An Essay Concerning Human Understanding*, 194.

11. Ibid., 415.

12. Plato, *Plato: Timaeus and Critias*, 57–59.

an innate distinction between body and soul involved more than the semantics of the word *psyche*. Greek pronouns, both personal and reflexive, began to find themselves placed in antithesis to the "body" or "corpse" in which the "ego" was thought of as residing.[13] So today we say: "The spirit is willing, but the flesh is weak." But the effects of this presupposed *internal* separation of spirit from flesh went beyond our self-perception, becoming *externalized* and generalized into real distinctions between the immaterial and the material, between human embodied reason and irrational animals. All of which have been ultimately based on the (usually tacit) assumption of a definitive separation of the spiritual from the earthly.

This, in effect, is what Locke takes for granted in the *Treatises*. He uses the term "Earth" as an abstract idea and not as a known, experienced, essential, material, living cosmic entity in an ever-evolving universe. Earth dissolves, disappears into the abstraction "Property"; owned, governed, and used by another abstract, "Man"; whose right to do so is based on another abstraction, "Reason." This "abstracted integration" is divorced from the specific life situations, feelings, and concrete results that govern and follow from the actions of real people. Above all, it is divorced from any attempt to anticipate or take into account the effects of ignoring the self's sensual experience of earthiness in favor of an abstracted image of Earth. How can we relate ourselves and the very real circumstances of our lives to an abstraction, "property," in which all experience of being an "earthling" is lost to another abstraction, "ownership"? And how can we take responsibility for the consequences of our manipulative behavior toward an "Earth" treated only as an abstracted scientific concept? Beautifully presented in color on our screens, it remains remote, untouchable, and unreachable.

From this perspective, I can understand why Havelock says that the split between the image-thinking of poetry, which fused subject with object in sympathetic self-identification, and the Platonic separation of objective knowledge from the knowing subject, ushered in a completely new stage in the development not only of the Greek but of the European mind.

> It announced the arrival of a new level of discourse which, as it
> became perfected, was to create in turn a new kind of experience
> of the world—the reflective, the scientific, the technological, the
> theological, the analytic.[14] [And, I would add, the manipulative.]

As the following chapter will demonstrate, it also ushered in a new political approach to lands and their indigenous oral cultures outside European

13. Havelock, *Preface to Plato*, 197–98.
14. Hallman, ed., *Ecotheology*, 266–67.

Christian dominions. This finds some of its clearest expressions in Locke's *Treatises* and their presupposition that colonization *required* that the "object, both human and other-than-human" be "torn out of context in living nature." In this you can see the beginnings of the effects of a perceived (not real) split between us and the natural world.[15]

However, the coupling of this with Homer's legacy of "heroic" warfare—no less enduring, and in its effects, intensified by the presumed split between us and the natural world—has created our most immediately destructive relationship with Earth. Through the influence and development of a global military-industrial complex, politics remains identified with soldiers, armies, and warfare controlled by government and economic systems that implicitly, and all too often explicitly, cultivate a view of other people and their natural environments solely in adversarial, competitive, and monetary terms. With such a mindset, the consequent destruction of Earth's creatures and natural resources is reduced to another abstraction, "collateral damage"—regarded as regrettable but inevitable and thereby unimportant in the great scheme of human "civilization."

15. La Chapelle, *Sacred Land, Sacred Sex, Rapture of the Deep*, 26.

6

Colonized Earth

*We Native people did not have the concept of private property in our
lexicon and the principles of private property were pretty much in conflict
with our value system. For example, you wouldn't see "No hunting" or
"No fishing" or "No Trespassing" signs in our territories. To a Native person
such signs would have been equivalent to "no breathing" because the air is
somebody's private property.*[1]

*Thus in the beginning all the World was America, and more so than that is
now; for no such thing as Money was anywhere known. Find out something
that hath the Use and Value of Money amongst his Neighbours, you shall
see the same man will begin presently to Enlarge his Possessions.*[2]

These two epigraphs define, in the clearest terms, what colonizing has meant
for the colonized, for the colonizers from Western cultures and for the complex totality of shared earthly life. Colonialists distinguish between their own
background and those countries where people live a non-proprietorial and
non-monetized relationship with Earth. And as money and property are the

1. Rajotte, *First Nations Faith and Ecology*, 29.
2. John Locke quoted in Laslett, *Locke*, 301.

54

distinguishing marks of their own societies, they presume the right to invade those countries and so "enlarge their own possessions." In pursuit of that aim, they have also assumed that they are entitled to slaughter or to enslave any indigenous peoples who resist them.

This clash of worldviews has meant that while precolonized peoples, like those Native Americans quoted in the first epigraph, regard themselves as part of a complex, interconnected community of living beings bound together by their shared dependence on natural resources, colonizers regarded them and their shared resources as an investment opportunity; as a means of enlarging land ownership and increasing the bank balances of individuals or corporate bodies like the East India Company. The latter worldview has "legitimated" extreme violence inflicted on precolonized peoples and their lands in ways that, as we now know, have affected and continue to affect the well-being of the whole earthly community. The present state of the Amazon rainforest and all its indigenous inhabitants, human and other-than-human, are both a reminder and a warning in this regard.

Locke implicitly acknowledges that the first epigraph above sums up the "original" human experience of life on Earth—the original condition in which God placed mankind. It is the first stage of the state of nature in which property is defined in naturalistic terms; one where the key concepts are freedom of one's person, labor, use, the right to subsistence, and the Law of Nature or God's will. For Locke, Native Americans provide a useful illustration of a stage preceding the transition to the institution of a political, property-owning society. And since, in Locke's time, North America was at this "first stage" of the state of nature, Europeans could rightly come and appropriate the land. The fact that they settled on it and put work into it, rather than living a nomadic existence, gave them, in Locke's eyes, more right to it than that held by the indigenous peoples.

> Thus Labour, in the beginning, gave a right of Property wherever anyone was pleased to employ it, upon what was common, which remained, a long while, the far greater part and yet more than Mankind makes use of.[3]

Locke also remarks that the gradual introduction of "Money" into society was the crucial factor in this transition to the colonizing enterprise of "Enlargement of Possessions." For *"before the desire of having more than Men needed"* had altered the intrinsic value of things, they

3. Ibid., 299.

had agreed, that a little piece of yellow Metal, which would keep
without wasting or decay, should be worth a great piece of Flesh,
or a whole heap of Corn.[4]

With respect to North America, this desire to have more than we need did
indeed alter the intrinsic, life sustaining value of its natural resources in ways
that endure up to the present day. "Flesh" and "corn" here stand proxy for all
colonized lands, providing a *raison d'être* for depriving the indigenous peoples
of the ownership of their native lands, excepting only the parts they actually
worked. So when Europeans arrived and appropriated the rest, the indigenous
peoples could not contest the colonizers' right to do so. If they did, they were
seen to be in a state of war in which they could, entirely legitimately, be killed
like wild animals. Furthermore, the colonizers could now claim financial re-
imbursement of the costs of war and so indemnify their losses. Not only did
they secure the lands and resources through physical force; they then used
those lands for financial gain to further "enlarge" their possessions. Then this
revenue could be and was used to consolidate their political and financial
power at home and abroad.[5]

This pattern of conduct has held true throughout recorded history
whenever and wherever empires were established. It characterized the Aztec
Empire in South America, the Egyptian and Babylonian Empires in the Near
East, the Roman Empire in western and eastern Europe, the Spanish Empire
in North and South America, the Dutch Empire in the East Indies and the
British Empire in Africa, India, America, and Australasia. These examples of
territorial expansion have been extensively chronicled and analyzed and are
now critiqued in our "post-imperial" age. As I continue to highlight the philosophical and religious mental categories used to justify the processes through
which colonized lands and their resources became seen and used as "property," it will become clear how this process has gradually changed our perceived
relationship with "earth" as a whole and not just with particular territories and
their inhabitants. The intrinsic connection between this development and the
use of money will be explored in the next chapter.

In pre-colonial America, which Locke epitomizes as "the beginning of
all the World," there was no categorizing of land and its creatures in monetary
terms and therefore no impetus to possess and accumulate property and its
surrogate, monetary wealth. Instead the territories, animal species, plant systems, and natural resources were recognized and valued for what they are in
themselves by "First Nations" peoples: as supporting the whole community of

---

4. Ibid., 294.

5. Duchrow and Hinkelammert, *Property for People, Not for Profit*, 61.

life, without discrimination or exclusion. This fundamental awareness of the unity between Earth's resource base and the lives of all its creatures defined the way of life of all nomadic peoples. As indeed it distinguished Abel the nomadic herder from Cain the settled farmer.

Peoples had first migrated from northern China across the Bering Strait land bridge to North America somewhere between 40,000 and 30,000 BCE. Their impact on the continent over the following millennia was very slight as they developed ways and means of relating to each other and to the land based upon a very simple and pragmatic understanding of their presence there. If they failed to take account of what the environment had to offer, how much it could give and at what times it was prepared to do so, they would simply die. This law held true not only for them but for every living thing around them. The plant world could not grow in the winter; the animal world too had to heed the changing of seasons. Otherwise they would die. If the people depleted the animal or plant resources of their immediate environment, their pain, suffering, and death could be expected to follow.[6]

When did this worldview begin to change? When did the concept of land as private property and with it, the use of money, become the norm? While there are different theories regarding its origins, it is certain that by the late eighth century BCE the mental category of "private" property had "gained ground" in Greece and in the whole of the ancient Near East. It is also certain that money originated around the same time, not yet in the form of coins but based on barter. Eventually this led to land and resources being valued in monetary terms and used by individuals or groups to accumulate more money. Aristotle distinguished two types of this "barter economy": one to supply households and the broader community with the goods needed to satisfy basic needs; the second, however, to *increase* monetary property for its own sake, in which buying and selling encouraged a more artificial form of acquisition.[7]

The gradual shift over time from the first to the second type of economy was noted by Aristotle, as were the differing motivations behind the second type which was designed to increase monetary property for its own sake. He described this as an "unnatural" economic form, one divorced from the realities of the natural world and motivated by human desire. In time it becomes an unrestrained desire to accumulate money; creating an illusion in the individual person of being able to acquire infinite "means of sustenance" and of pleasure, and implicitly, living forever thereby. Ultimately, the striving for more property through monetary mechanisms was seen by him as based on

6. Rajotte, *First Nations Faith and Ecology*, 1–2.

7. Duchrow and Hinkelammert, *Property for People, Not for Profit*, 5.

a desire that transcends the individually desired object; the desire for eternal life.[8]

This mental category of "desire for eternal life" underpinned the "unnatural" form of economy designed to accumulate money. It remains a dominant feature of the hereditary right of succession from one generation to another within property-owning classes. In its religious form, it became the explicitly declared motivation within Christian Europe for the acquisition of colonial territories. Quite simply, just as accumulating more property meant more money "saved" for future generations, the colonizing process was categorized as accumulating moral, "heavenly" capital in terms of "souls saved." The desire and opportunity "to save souls" through the spread of the Roman Catholic Church meant that popes legitimized and blessed the colonial enterprise. Sixty-nine Papal Bulls endorsing colonial expansion, generally obtained at the request of Kings, show the importance of this religious legitimation.

In 1452, in the Bull *Dum diversas*, Pope Martin V addressed the king of Portugal:

> In the name of our apostolic authority, we grant you . . . the full and entire faculty of invading, conquering, expelling and reigning over all the kingdoms, the duchies . . . of the Saracens, of pagans, and of all infidels wherever they may be found; of reducing their inhabitants to perpetual slavery, of appropriating to yourself these kingdoms and all their possessions, for your own use and that of your successors.[9]

This horrific program was "justified" on the religious grounds of "saving souls" that were assumed, by their very nature, to be "immaterial" and "unearthly." Appeal to these mental categories manifested an implicit and sometimes explicit disdain of earth, of "earthy" peoples and of their "pagan" earth-focused lives and rituals. With such justifying concepts in place, it became morally right as well as economically politic to extend territorial boundaries to other countries and continents.

On that declared basis, Spain and Portugal initiated the conquest and colonization of the Amerindian territories. Beginning with Columbus in 1492, this placed European Christians at the center of a burgeoning worldwide colonial system. Subsequent events like the Reformation, the Enlightenment, and the scientific revolution helped northern Europe displace Spain. The Protestant nations, principally represented colonially by England and Holland, were

8. Ibid.
9. Balasuriya, *Planetary Theology*, 122.

part of this displacement, eventually relocating Catholicism to the periphery of the Christian world.

From the start, however, the role played by a religious rather than a fiscal mental category of "eternal life" added an unimpeachably righteous impetus to military invasion of the pagan, oral cultures of the "First Nations." "Spiritual conquest" and "extirpation of idolatry" were routinely invoked in the Spanish invasion and colonization of America. To read the historical accounts of what this actually meant for the indigenous peoples is to revisit one of the most violent, deathly, and destructive enterprises in the history of humanity. But then these were justified on the grounds of those people being "less than" or "other than" fully human; that is, Christian "souls":

> It was ideologically impossible for the Spanish crown to conceive the conquest and colonization of America in terms other than missionary evangelization. It could not articulate the legitimacy of its colonial dominion exclusively from a political or economic perspective. What for other modern empires might be possible, namely, to control the instruments of political and economic power while allowing the dominated peoples spiritual solace for their troubled subjectivity in their native religiosity, was absolutely out of the question for sixteenth century Spain. The spiritual conquest and the "extirpation of idolatry" were essential elements of the Spanish conquest and colonization of the Americas. They constituted their ideological matrix and symbolic configuration.[10]

Yet from the start there were prophetic voices that questioned the colonial process and its disastrous effects on indigenous peoples and their lands. Martinez-Vazquez cites Bartolomé de la Casas, born in Seville in 1484, who came to America in 1502 to help in the established family business of farming and trading. After being ordained a priest in Rome in 1507 he returned to his Amerindian lands and started to question the unjust treatment of the indigenous peoples. He saw that while the colonizer gained control over the colonized through violence, the colonial discourse of superiority, providential messianism and call to evangelization gave ideological support to the violence. In his *Devastation of the Indies* he notes how economic reasons superseded religious motivations: that the reason for killing and destroying such an infinite number of souls is that the Christians' ultimate aim is acquiring gold and "swelling themselves with riches" in a very brief time.

> It should be kept in mind that their insatiable greed and ambition, the greatest ever seen in the world, is the cause of their villainies.

10. Martinez-Vazquez, "Bartolome De Las Casas," 203–5.

> And also, those lands are so rich and felicitous, the native peoples
> so meek and patient, so easy to subject, that our Spaniards have
> no more consideration for them than beasts. But I should not say
> "than beasts," for thanks be to God, they have treated beasts with
> some respect; I should say instead like excrement on the public
> squares.[11]

During and after Locke's lifetime, as earlier in Las Casas's time, the economic
arguments in support of colonialism outstripped any religious consideration.
As "New" England was being transformed by economic and population
growth, communities that had been largely based on subsistence farming
as well as mutual trade and aid within the British Empire were developing
competitive and differentiated economies, politicized factions and a culture of
competitive individualism.

> This growth was due partly to the industry and high birthrate of
> colonists, but also to the expropriation of Native American lands,
> the destruction of their way of life, and the labor and suffering of
> African American slaves.[12]

Yet for some Puritans like Jonathan Edwards (1703–1758), physical realities
were always representative of spiritual realities. He lived in a world framed by
God's work of redemption that reached from the beginning of the world to its
end and beyond. He understood this work as an apocalyptic struggle between
God and the forces of evil; unfolding as foretold in the Bible, particularly in
the Book of Revelation. He identified himself and Protestant churches with
the faithful elect while (reversing the categories of the 1452 Papal Bull) Roman Catholicism, Islam, other "natural" indigenous religions and the political
powers aligned with them were "Satan's visible empire upon earth".[13] We have
already seen how this Christian religious categorization reflected and supported attitudes and destructive changes to the pre-Reformation landscape
in England and Ireland. Religious mental categories, in this case those of absolute good and evil, continued to underpin and justify the external drive to
conquer "Earth" in all its forms.

   John Wesley visited Georgia in 1735. His response to what he found
there was influenced both by the effects of this religiously motivated war on
the poor, excluded, and enslaved peoples of North America and their lands
and by its legitimation as the civilizing mission of Christian Europe. He did
not presuppose that the Christian West was the repository of wisdom for how

11. Ibid., 207.
12. Schweitzer, "Jonathan Edwards," 243–44.
13. Ibid., 244–45.

to live in harmony with nature. Indeed his goal in going to Georgia was to learn from the native peoples how to carry out the prescriptions of Acts 2 and 4 concerning the sharing of goods; though he did admit to friends that his chief desire was "to save my own soul."

In this cause he supposed he would live on "water and the fruits of the earth"; hoping to banish from his mind the desire for externals that beset him everywhere in England by learning from the Native Americans how to live by "having all things in common" (Acts 2:42). "What a guard is here against that root of all evil, the love of money, and all the vile attractions that spring from it!"[14]

As it happened, Wesley was not able to fulfill his dream because the head of the Georgia colony, Oglethorpe, forced him to devote his time to the spiritual direction of the English colonists and serve as Oglethorpe's assistant in managing the colony's affairs. Many years later, in a homily on the Sermon on the Mount, Wesley recalled the features of Native American life that first drew him to Georgia:

> The Heathen desires nothing more than plain food to eat, plain raiment to put on; and he seeks this only from day to day. . . . They "lay up for themselves no treasures upon earth"; no stores of purple, fine linen, gold or silver. But how do the Christians observe what they profess to receive as a command of the most high God? Not at all!

His appreciation of the virtues not only of Native Americans but also of African cultures undercuts one of the principal legitimations of emerging empires: the so-called civilizing mission of Europe. Instead, his appreciation of the virtues of those indigenous cultures led to broadsides against British imperial designs in India:

> Look into that large country, Indostan. There are Christians and heathens too. Which have more justice, mercy and truth? . . . Which have desolated whole countries and clogged the rivers with dead bodies? O sacred name of Christian! How profaned! O earth, earth, earth! How dost thou groan under the villainies of thy Christian inhabitants!

And he excoriates the slave trade centered on the Caribbean colonies and their sugar plantations:

> First, it were better that all those islands should remain uncultivated for ever, yea, it were more desirable that they were altogether

14. Jennings, "John Wesley," 259.

sunk in the depth of the sea, than that they should be cultivated at so high a price as the violation of justice, mercy and truth.[15]

Yet, "cultivation" of land for profit had been and remained the basic argument for colonization and for "*a right of property*" put forward by Locke:

> An acre of Land that bears here Twenty Bushels of Wheat, and another in America, which, with the same Husbandry, would do the like are, without doubt, of the same natural intrinsic Value. But yet the Benefit Mankind receives from the one, in a year, is worth 5l [£5], and from the other possibly not worth a Penny, if all the profit an Indian received from it were to be valued and sold here. . . . From all which is evident, that though the things of nature are given in common, yet Man (by being master of himself, and Proprietor of his own Person, and the actions or labour of it) had still in himself the great Foundation of Property; and that which made up the great part of what he applied to the Support or Comfort of his being, when Invention and the Arts had improved the conveniences of Life, was perfectly his own, and did not belong in common to others. . . . Thus Labour, in the Beginning, gave a right of Property, wherever anyone was pleased to imply it, upon what was common.[16]

In the nineteenth century this "foundation text" was incorporated into *The Founders' Constitution* of the United States: more or less defining Earth as human "property" by right of labor in all Western constitutions. Humankind is, according to Locke, a property-owning species. All human rights derive from property. Therefore, the sole purpose of the State is the protection of this hypostatized property. We find the same development in the French Declaration of the Rights of Man at the time of the French Revolution in 1789. Drawing on Roman law, it designates property as an inviolable and divine right (Article 17). But the absolutism of property is given its most unequivocal wording in Article 544 of the Code Napoleon which has formed the basis of nearly all civil codes since that time:

> Property is the absolute right to utilize and possess things, provided that one does not use them in a way that is contrary to the laws and statutes.[17]

---

15. Ibid., 259, 263, 265.
16. Laslett, *Locke*, 298–99.
17. Duchrow and Hinkelammert, *Property for People, Not for Profit*, 78.

Locke's statement legitimating human government of Earth was made at a time when England's empire was gradually expanding in immediate conflict with the existing imperial powers of its time, particularly Spain and the Netherlands. The English expansion was primarily directed towards countries outside Europe with North America as its most important goal. A further expansion to the Far East was already under way, aimed in particular at India. Simultaneously, England was striving for a monopoly in the most profitable trade of this period, the slave trade, previously in the hands of Spain. Locke himself had invested his personal fortune in the slave trade, as Voltaire did after him.[18]

This overall view and brief analysis of some few features of the broad historical canvas inscribed "colonialism" serves to highlight what postcolonialist scholars call the "discourses of colonialism": that is, the beliefs, cultural trends, and mental categories or symbolic configurations clustered around Earth as "land" that legitimated European colonization from the fifteenth century onwards. One such key concept, that of property, supported, as we have seen, by Reformed biblical discourse, was fundamental to British colonization of North America. In South America, where Spain and Portugal played the defining role of colonizer, the discourse centered on the Roman Catholic religious understanding of missionary evangelization. In other words, it was based on the religious identity and "superiority" of the colonizer and the presumed religious inferiority of the colonized.[19]

Demonstrating a disdain similar to that of Plato for such oral cultures, Locke's writings disclose historic approaches to land, property and money that were closely linked to each other and still are to this day. The boundless accumulation of monetary wealth still appears to create the illusion of accumulating infinite "means of sustenance" and "means of pleasure"; and thereby "living" forever. Striving for more and more possession of land/earth as property or money, both individual and corporate bodies are blind to the community of earthly life and so are increasingly destructive of it.

The truth of this is now globally evident. It has played out historically as violent military and destructive colonization of indigenous peoples' lands followed by their ecological devastation. While it is true that other forms of colonization have taken place in which groups of people have fled from persecution, discrimination, and poverty in their homelands in search of a better life, they have not been the norm. In general, rather than regarding colonized lands and their indigenous inhabitants as the refuge of and resource base for the flourishing of all forms of life, colonizers have viewed them solely as an

18. Ibid., 44–45.
19. Martinez-Vazquez, "Bartolome De Las Casas," 203–5.

enlargement of individual possessions and, as we shall see in the following chapter, as a primary source of monetary gain.

This approach and its consequences define what Gary Snyder now sees as "America." It can be read as confirming the "success" of Locke's vision of its lands and inhabitants as "property" to be used solely as a potential source of monetary wealth:

> I'll say this real clearly, because it seems that it has to be said over and over again. There is no place to flee to in the U.S. There is no "country" that you can go and lay back in. There is no quiet place in the woods. . . . The surveyors are there with their orange plastic tape, the bulldozers are down the road warming up their engines, the real estate developers have got it all on the wall with pins in it, the county supervisors are in the back room drinking coffee with the real estate subdividers . . . and the forest service is just about to let out a big logging contract to some logging company.[20]

What this describes is the gradual destruction of Gaia/Earth through the weapons of war, commerce, and industrialization. And with it, the loss of our own sense of wholeness and well-being as earth creatures. Within our most affluent societies we grow up detached from our biological roots deep in the natural world and from our psychic relationships with diverse life forms. Instead, we live in a "humans only" world where it is assumed each of us acts as a mind inside the limits of a body. Trapped there, we are caught in the very thing we fear most—our mortality.

---

20. La Chapelle, *Sacred Land, Sacred Sex, Rapture of the Deep*, 130.

7

Monetized Earth

A crucial point here is that the introduction of money in effect suspends the spoilage proviso, which says that we can take no more from the bounty of nature than we can use before it spoils. For now by industrious labor we can acquire more than we can use but exchange the surplus for money (or claims to valuable things of various kinds) and thereby accumulate larger and larger holdings in land and natural resources, or whatever.[1]

Money allows a man to fairly possess more land than he himself can use the product of, by receiving in exchange for the overplus, Gold and Silver, which may be hoarded up without injury to any one, these metalls not spoiling or decaying in the hands of the possessor. This partage of things, in an inequality of private possessions, men have made practicable out of the bounds of Societie, and without compact, only by putting a value on gold and silver and tacitly agreeing in the use of Money.[2]

An estimated 70m hectares of agricultural land—or 5% of Africa—has been sold or leased to western investors since 2000. . . . Investors have spent between $5bn and $15bn on farmland. They expect that investment

1. Rawls, *Lectures on the History of Political Philosophy*, 149.
2. John Locke quoted in Laslett, *Locke*, 302.

to double by 2015. . . . Nyikaw Ochalba, of the Anuak people in Ethiopia, said:"land-grabbing" is accelerating at a rate not seen since colonial times.[3]

The first crucial point about property argued for by Locke (in the second epigraph above) was the labor cost theory of value: that is, that the labor we put into land is the property we have in our own person to which no one else has a right. This was a decisive argument for colonizing "America"; where "a king might be rich in land not yet improved by labor and so be housed, fed, and clad worse than a day laborer in England.[4] Labor is the great "Foundation" of the right to property. But there is a proviso: this right of use and so of property is not an exclusive one. Others also have the same right.[5]

The second proviso made by Locke is the one mentioned above: the spoilage clause. Because God is always sole proprietor of the Earth and its resources, to take more than we need from them is to waste and destroy part of God's property. This is dealt with, according to Locke, by the introduction of money. On that basis, if labor produces more from the land than is needed, the surplus can be sold and the money so raised is then available to acquire larger land holdings. The value of those lands is subsequently based on the value of the "base metals": gold and silver. They, or rather those who value them, also set the value of the "overplus" or surplus production. The use of such market terms for the abundance of Earth's produce implicitly devalued its original life support value as perceived by the indigenous owners of the property. They produced or used what was sufficient for their needs, but not for the greed of those who ousted them from their homeland.

The observable long-term effects of Locke's arguments for valuing and acquiring "property" and its products are noted in the third epigraph. But the game has moved on still further. Present day investors who expect their money to double through land acquisition do not expect to labor or to live on the agricultural land themselves in order to produce food surpluses to be sold at a profit on world markets. Their investment is purely a monetary transaction intended to "make" more money by buying "shares" in land from a property owning company: one based not in Africa but in a Western financial district or tax haven. That company will then "generate profit" for the investors by

3. *The Guardian*, June 26, 2012.

4. Laslett, *Locke*, 296f.

5. Ibid., 291.

paying an African-based subsidiary to employ workers at the lowest possible subsistence wage whose labor will provide raw materials for sale on world markets at the highest price available. Then these will be outsourced to countries where manufacturing is less expensive and the products sold worldwide.

Before Locke and since, some investors used their money to buy large tracts of land and property in their homelands. Many of these magnificent residences are preserved as historic monuments to an elegant and affluent lifestyle. Now such investors are more likely to buy islands on which to enjoy a secluded and privileged lifestyle while building major city conurbations that command ever-increasing prices and a dependable income stream. It is also the case that Aristotle's "property accumulation" now means generating or accumulating money at a distance: that is, in cyberspace. Here there is no tangible or direct relationship with land and consequently no concern for its "spoilage." And therefore no need to take account of the knock-on effects on those indigenous inhabitants, human and other-than-human, whose lives depend on that land's actual soil- and water-based resources.

Instead, those resources and those of the seas surrounding them are used as "tokens" to accumulate wealth by betting on the rise and fall of prices for crops and products now considered solely as means to that end—such as oil. A purely notional chain of "monetary wealth" production now binds the Earth's resources to the money markets and to those who manipulate them: while at the same time it keeps the marketeers at a physical, mental, and moral distance from the effects of their exploitation of land and its inhabitants. The current mental category of "futures," under which a large part of the world's food market functions today, distances these marketeers even further in time as well as place from the current effects of notional rises or falls in commodity prices.

An integral component of this notional chain binding us to Earth and Earth to our way of thinking is the *idea* of money. By the seventeenth century, mining for "Gold and Silver" had created currencies in "precious" metals whose notional value set the prices of land and its store of commodities. Tons of earth were removed and discarded as "overburden" in order to mine this underground treasure. In Locke's England, the monetary system of its Empire was largely based on metallic gold that itself had become the standard as well as the bearer of value in monetary exchange. "Coins of the realm" included those looted from Spanish silver fleets on their journey back to Europe from the Americas. But there was a "hierarchy" of metals that held firm; ranging from the lowest in value, tin, upwards through copper and silver to gold. However, as gold was rare, the only true English coin was silver—crowns, half-crowns, shillings and sixpences. As Locke himself remarked: "Silver is the instrument and measure of commerce in all the civilized and trading parts of the world."[6]

But this civilized "instrument and measure" was then in deep crisis. The crisis was caused by criminals whose persistent activity, such as "clipping" silver coins, counterfeiting them, and smuggling bullion, led to the markets being distorted and the coinage's value being either inflated or deflated. This, as Locke saw, led to profound social disorder. He helped organize the struggle against it by arranging for Isaac Newton to leave Cambridge and become Warden of the Mint. From there, Newton became the detector, interrogator, and prosecutor of the criminals, helping to fill Newgate Prison and provide employment for the hangman at Tyburn.

Why did Newton and Locke react so severely? By 1695 it was clear to them and to Lowndes—the Secretary of the Treasury—that the English coin was "physically crippled and not standard." And the international market was taking note of this fact. The clipping of coin was operating outside the state's control and indeed, *against* the state. For Locke, at a time that seemed ripe for a new world-power hierarchy with England at the top, civil government had its origin and end in the regulation of money. But a domestic "fix" would underestimate the enemy, for the threat was worldwide. And if England could not represent the interests of the world market, then it would not be able to claim the legitimacy of its rule. Such was the political context behind the coinage debate.[7]

That is why Locke considered the monetary crimes of clipping and counterfeiting so serious as to warrant capital punishment. While he was now tolerant of religious deviation he was almost religiously devoted to the quantitative and substantial "integrity" of silver and gold. So much so, says Caffentzis, that in his writings at the time, violators of the "body" of money became the real "robbers of the faith" in his demonology:

> Thus, according to his Letter concerning Toleration, a pagan should be permitted to sacrifice a calf to his gods in the middle of London, and even "devil worship" and idolatry should be given free rein so long as the worshippers do not violate the laws of civil society; but tampering with the coinage should be considered a capital crime of the most detestable nature.[8]

In Locke's *Further Considerations concerning Toleration* he uses a religious analogy to drive home his point:

6. Caffentzis, *Clipped Coins, Abused Words and Civil Government*, 18.

7. Ibid., 19–22.

8. Ibid., 46.

The use and end of the public stamp is only to be a guard and voucher of the quality of silver which men contract for; and the injury done to the public faith, in this point, is that by which in-clipping and false coining heightens the robbery into treason.[9]

Such a view, says Caffentzis, represents a momentous transformation in intellectual perspective and social policy. Clearly the locale of heresy has shifted from private religious conviction to public monetary faith. Simultaneously, a new "center of evil" and a new "thanatocracy" was founded; for coin clipping and counterfeiting were now raised from the ranks of petty crime to the level of a semantic heresy against the state, one far more dangerous than reading the Bible backwards or conversing with one's cat.[10]

This startling shift in mental categorization brings us to what Deborah Valenze calls "the social life of money." Seventeenth-century people like Locke recognized, she said, that money sustained an abundance of representations and practices, and within the nascent discipline of political economy the "idea" of money was a matter of considerable discussion. Unrecognized in a typical account of money today is the shadowy persistence of an abstract quality projected onto money that is rendered particularly powerful by factors such as a user's distance from centers of power or the legitimacy conferred upon a particular practice by the weight of custom.

> Money can move between concrete form and abstract idea at any time, entering into intellectual tasks, such as measuring and comparing things along a numerical scale, or relating different objects involved in transactions to a common scale of value. In the final analysis, as sociologist Geoffrey Ingham has argued, money becomes simply "a conceptual scheme for the measurement of value," which lies behind any particular form that it might take as a means of payment.[11]

This dual monetary identity, as both concrete form and abstract idea on a common scale of value, is so much part of modern society that we take it for granted. Yet it marks a major phase change in our relationship with earth and our relationship with money—or rather, with what Caffentzis calls "the semantic idea of money." What kind of idea is it and what do monetary terms actually signify?

According to Locke's categorizing, the original kind of property was a *substance*: Homer's cattle, wine and oil; the Bible's sheep, corn and bread . . . a

9. Ibid., 46.
10. Ibid., 46–47.
11. Valenze, *The Social Life of Money*, 21.

stuff or a thing with powers to ease our pain and enhance our pleasure. But is *money* a substance? *Gold* is money and gold is a substance:

> The ideas that make up our complex idea of gold are yellowness, great weight, ductility, fusibility, and solubility in aqua regia, &c., all united together in an unknown substratum; all which ideas are nothing else but so many relations to other substances, and are not really in the gold considered in itself, though they depend on those real and primary qualities of its internal constitution, whereby it has a fitness differently to operate, and to be operated on by other substances.[12]

But, says Caffentzis, money is *not* gold or silver or diamonds. What transformed these substances into money is another idea. Both "fancy or tacit agreement" put value on the substance and take it as "the universal barter, or exchange."

> Money is an idea of substance plus something else—a value men attribute to a substance that is not in it, a willingness to accept an equality between it and another object that is not in it either—a mixed mode. It is this non-substantial aspect of the complex of ideas that creates the mystery of money.[13]

This is as good a definition and example of a "mental category" as I can find. And one that has proved and still is impossible to shatter. For even though Western capitalism no longer takes the value of gold as the "standard" for its currencies, in the present economic climate of debased currencies, gold prices continue to soar. We continue to attribute a value to it that is not inherent in it; and are willing to accept an equality between it and currencies that is not *in* it either.

Similarly, in the Stock Exchanges of the "First World," "Africa" is not seen as an earthly resource base of land, seas, rivers, oceans, and atmosphere that sustains the life of all its inhabitants. Instead, it is seen as a source of monetary gain. The shared natural dependence of its indigenous creatures on its unique life support systems is ignored in that they are valued solely in financial terms that form the basis for market transactions elsewhere. Whereas their true value lies in the fact that they are the interactive, unique, and essential life resources on which all life forms within the natural world depend.

> Market activity created what anthropologists and historians have identified as monetization: a process that involves more than

12. Locke, *An Essay Concerning Human Understanding*, 198.
13. Caffentzis, *Clipped Coins, Abused Words and Civil Government*, 75–76.

simply adopting specie as tokens of exchange. This larger definition views money as permeating social thought, introducing a new
"way of organizing and of thinking about many crucial matters." In
particular, money imbues all things with its trademark character
of fungibility, suggesting interchangeability with anything else.[14]

This is what defines "monetized earth": a process through which we have
learned to disdain it unless we can imbue it with some monetary "value," using it as a mere accessory to the property system. Thomas Hobbes saw how
the very attributes of human power in society were permeated by this thinking
and illustrated this in vivid terms:

> The Value or WORTH of a man, is as of all other things, his Price,
> that is to say, so much as would be given for the use of his Power
> and therefore is not absolute; but a thing dependent on the need
> and judgment of another. . . . As in other things, so in men, not the
> seller but the buyer determines the Price. For let a man (as most
> men do) rate themselves at the highest Value they can; yet their
> true Value is no more than it is esteemed by others.[15]

It should come as no surprise, then, says Valenze, that early modern people
often measured their world and even themselves in monetary terms. The
commitment of enormous resources to colonial and commercial ventures, the
creation of capital markets and the birth of consumer societies, tapped into a
marked human propensity to use and think about money and financial instruments for personal gain. A concurrent wellspring of consumer commodities
indicated a growing participation in exchange relations advanced by the use of
money and credit in the seventeenth century. Popular commodities (imported
from the colonies) like tobacco, sugar products, coffee, tea, and chocolate
joined a list of household and personal durables that declined in price and
broadened in availability even as they supported a competitive, individualis-
tic strain of economic behavior. Money cannot be understood, says Valenze,
apart from its social context in history.[16]

And neither can it be understood apart from the mental categories that
surround it and endorse the ways in which we use it and in turn are used by it.
One very powerful category has been that of usury; that is, of charging interest on a loan. In practice, this makes money from money. Or it may take the
form of an agreement by which money itself can lose money. In the latter case,
it's called "debt." I shall go into this at greater length in the following chapter.

14. Valenze, *The Social Life of Money*, 12.
15. Ibid., 12–13.
16. Ibid., 12–15.

Here I want to highlight the role played by indebtedness in all the European colonial expeditions and the consequent attitudes to colonized lands, their products and their peoples.

As I have already pointed out, the expenses incurred in colonizing expeditions were loaned at interest. In 1518, for example, Cortes, heavily in debt, managed to have himself appointed commander of a Spanish expedition to the Mexican mainland. However, he had no money to defray the expenses. But some merchant friends who heard that he had obtained his command lent him four thousand gold pesos. Then the expedition was cancelled by the governor. But Cortes ignored him, sailed and burnt his boats on landing. Three years later, through some of the most ingenious, ruthless, brilliant, and utterly dishonorable behavior ever recorded of a military leader, Cortes had his victory. The Mexican imperial treasury was secured and the time had come for it to be divided among the Spanish survivors.

> The result was outrage. The officers connived to sequester most of the gold and the troops learned that they would receive only fifty to eighty pesos each. What's more, the better part of their shares was immediately seized again by the officers in their capacity as creditors—since Cortes had insisted that the men be billed for any replacement equipment and medical care they had received during the siege. Most found they had actually lost money on the deal. ... Then Spanish merchants arrived charging vastly inflated prices for basic necessities.[17]

These were the men, says David Graeber, who ended up in control of the colonies, establishing local administrations, taxes, and labor regimes. Now the relationship between the daring adventurer on the one hand—the gambler willing to take any sort of risk—and, on the other, the careful financier whose entire operations are organized around producing steady inexorable growth of income, lies at the heart of what we now call "capitalism." All of which explains why the Christian church had to wrestle with it. It was not just a philosophical question; it was a matter of moral rivalry, for money always has the potential to become a moral imperative in itself.

> Human relations become a matter of cost-benefit calculation. Clearly this is the way the conquistadores viewed the worlds that they set out to conquer. It is the peculiar feature of modern capitalism to create social structures that essentially force us to think this way.[18]

17. Graeber, Debt, 317–19.
18. Ibid., 319–20.

This was another decisive shift in human self-imagery: from accepting our shared dependence on Earth and its resources to perceiving them in terms of monetized property to be possessed, bartered, sold, and bought by the privileged few. The conceptual basis for this shift involved a move from categorizing land as the provider of sustenance for its own inhabitants, human and more-than-human, to categorizing it primarily as a producer of monetary gain. True, by the seventeenth century the now familiar polestars of monetary life—State finances, commercial ventures, and private investment strategies—were as yet imperfectly constructed and heavily contested in a flurry of debates about the "idea" of money. So *Ecclesiastes* was cited by Locke to remind readers that "Money answereth all things." But he also believed that this required establishing its coinage value as equal to the value of its precious metal. This desire for "honest" value was the basis for his attempt to deal with illicit coin production that threatened to undermine the power of the Crown's Mint. By joining the Crown's authority to coinage and applying the penalty of death to counterfeiting, he introduced a new emphasis on and direction in State control to counter the disorderliness of the previous half-century.[19]

Up to now I have stressed Locke's emphasis on the relationship between labor and the private appropriation of land in the development of the notion of property. But the eventual hegemony of money not only allowed the accumulation of wealth but also stopped its being defined and bounded by use or scarcity. For Locke, scarcity was not natural. With money a man could own more land and produce more than he needed for his own necessities. Indeed, as Aristotle discerned, he could accumulate wealth in a quasi-eternal form. One that he might or might not share with others.[20]

Also, by this time money had become a political instrument rather than a moral question. Graeber notes that under the newly emerging capitalist order, the logic of money was granted autonomy, and military and political power organized around it. Luther had begun his career as a reformer in 1520 with fiery campaigns against usury; in fact, one of his objections to the sale of Church indulgences was that it was itself a form of spiritual usury. However, he soon realized that he'd unleashed a genie that threatened to turn the whole world upside down when more radical reformers argued that the poor were not morally obliged to repay the interest on usurious loans.

The Swiss Protestant reformer Zwingli was even more explicit. God, he argued, gave us the divine law: to love thy neighbor as thyself. If we kept it, humans would give freely to one another and private property would not exist. However, Jesus excepted, no human being has been able to live up to this pure

19. Valenze, *The Social Life of Money*, 20, 41.
20. Caffentzis, *Clipped Coins, Abused Words and Civil Government*, 50.

communistic standard. Therefore, God has also given us a second, inferior human law, to be enforced by the civil authorities by which we can at least follow the lead of the apostle Paul, who said: "Pay all men what you owe."

Soon afterwards, Calvin was to reject the blanket ban on usury and, by 1650, almost all Protestant denominations had come to agree with his position that a reasonable rate of interest was not sinful. If one looks at how all this was justified, says Graeber, two things jump out. First, Protestant thinkers all continued to make the old medieval argument about *interesse*: that "interest" is really compensation for the money that the lender *would* have made had he been able to place his money in some more profitable investment. Originally applied to commercial loans, increasingly this was applied to all loans, so that far from being "unnatural," the "growth" of money was now treated as completely expected. All money was assumed to be "capital."

> Second, the assumption that usury is something that one properly practices on one's enemies, and therefore, by extension, that all commerce partakes something of the nature of war, never entirely disappears. Calvin, for instance, denied that Deuteronomy only referred to the Amalekites; clearly, he said, it meant that usury was acceptable when dealing with Syrians or Egyptians; indeed with all nations with whom the Jews traded. The result of opening the gates was, at least tacitly, to suggest that one could now treat anyone, even a neighbour, as a foreigner. One need only observe how European merchant adventurers of the day actually were treating foreigners, in Asia, Africa and the Americas, to understand what this might mean in practice.[21]

The first and most obvious parallel with today is that individuals' immoderate and apparently insatiable delight in monetary wealth can only be satisfied at the expense of others' welfare; human and other-than-human alike. As in the fourth century BCE, when individuals in our free market capitalist culture pay inordinate attention to the pursuit of wealth it means that many other groups are forced to work in intolerable conditions; or that they find themselves bankrupt, starving or out of work; and that as land and sea habitats are ravaged by industrial processes and machinery, our planetary resource systems go into decline.

Globally, major corporate bodies that neither recognize nor act upon moral criteria that would prevent them from harming others are instead legally compelled by pragmatic concern for their own interests to *cause* harm when the benefits to its shareholders of doing so outweigh the costs. Oil

21. Graeber, *Debt*, 322–23.

exploration, for example, tends to be viewed as the inevitable (and therefore implicitly acceptable) consequence of corporate activity. In the technical jargon of economics its effects are "externalities": that is, they affect a third party who has not consented to or played any role in carrying out a transaction. When such an "externality" affects people and the environment badly, executives have no authority to consider those effects unless they might negatively affect the corporation itself. In practice, that means ignoring any bad "external" effects resulting from corporations' relentless and legally required pursuit of self-interest.[22]

Globally, such "external effects" are now manifest, not least in the piles of inedible "goods" that grow ever higher in refuse dumps sited (far from corporate headquarters) in the slums of South America, Africa, China, and India. And in the slum dwellings of those who work to create products that quickly end as "refuse." They have been created through the power of our abstracting, pattern-making brain that has reached its apogee in the "abstraction" of "money" from all that makes earthly life possible. Calling a forest "timber," fish "resources," the wilderness "raw material," indigenous peoples "foreigners," licenses us to treat them accordingly. It certainly bars the experience of Earth described by William Wordsworth as:

> A presence that disturbs me with the joy
> Of elevated thoughts; a sense sublime
> Of something far more deeply interfused,
> Whose dwelling is the light of setting suns,
> And the round ocean and the living air,
> And the blue sky, and in the mind of man:
> A motion and a spirit, that impels
> All thinking things, all objects of all thought,
> And rolls through all things.[23]

22. Bakan, *The Corporation*, 60–61.
23. Wordsworth, "Lines Composed a Few Miles above Tintern Abbey."

8

Devalued Earth

*"Usury," argued Aristotle, "means the birth of money from money, [and]
is applied to the breeding of money, because the offspring resembles
the parent. Wherefore of all modes of making money this is the most
unnatural."*[1]

Aristotle describes two types of economy distinguished from one another by
how money is used. The first is where households and the broader community
use it as a means of exchanging the goods needed to satisfy basic needs and
enhance the quality of life (*oikonomike*). The second is where some individuals, having accumulated money, regard it as a property that can be increased
through usury (*kapilike*); buying and selling as part of an artificial form of
acquisition (*khremastike*). Aristotle agreed with Plato in citing human desire
(*epithymia*) as a motive for creating this second "unnatural" form. The accumulation of money for its own sake, without the production or direct exchange
of goods, creates the illusion of accumulating infinite "means of sustenance"
and of pleasure, thereby living forever. Employing money through lending in
order to accumulate more money endows it with regenerative power. Individuals who chase after this "groundless illusion" contribute to the destruction
of community.[2]

1. Valenze, *The Social Life of Money*, 54.
2. Duchrow and Hinkelammert, *Property for People, Not for Profit*, 5.

Today, the truth of this is evident in that it has brought major world economies into recession. So how did the practice of usury arise? What groups of people and what distinctive cultural interactions gave substance and prestige to the mental category now known as "interest"? The notion of adding it to consumer loans not only predates Aristotle but appears to predate writing. Anthropologist David Graeber ascribes its beginnings to Mesopotamian administrators who invented it as a way of financing the caravan trade. It was needed because the river valleys of ancient Mesopotamia were extraordinarily fertile, producing huge surpluses of grain and other foodstuffs as well as supporting enormous numbers of livestock. But they were almost completely lacking in stone, wood, metal, and even the silver used as money. All had to be imported. Temples, as vast industrial complexes, developed the custom of advancing goods to local merchants who would then set sail to sell them overseas. Interest was the way for a Temple to take its share of the resulting profits. Once established the principle quickly spread. Before long, we find not only commercial loans, but also consumer loans—usury in the classical sense:

> By c2400 BCE it already appears to have been common practice on the part of local officials, or wealthy merchants, to advance loans on collateral to peasants who were in financial trouble and begin to appropriate their possessions if they were unable to pay. It usually started with grain, sheep, goats and furniture, then moved on to fields and houses, or, alternately or ultimately, family members. . . . The effects were such that they often threatened to rip society apart.[3]

By the time of the Hebrew prophets, the Judean economy was already beginning to develop the same kind of debt crises that had long been common in Mesopotamia. Especially in years of bad harvests, the poor became indebted to rich neighbors or to wealthy moneylenders in the towns, losing titles to their fields, and becoming tenants on what had once been their own land. In 444 BCE the prophet Nehemiah, a Jew born in Babylon and former cupbearer to the Persian Emperor, was appointed governor of his native Judea. There he found himself surrounded by impoverished peasants unable to pay taxes and creditors carrying off the children of the poor:

> Some also there were that said, "We have mortgaged our lands, vineyards and houses, that we might buy corn, because of the dearth."

> There were also those that said: "We have borrowed money for the king's tribute, and that upon our lands and vineyards."

3. Graeber, *Debt*, 64–65.

> "Yet now our flesh is as the flesh of our brethren, our children as their children: and lo, we bring into bondage our sons and daughters, and some of our daughters are brought under bondage already: neither is it in our power to redeem them; for other men have our lands and vineyards."
>
> And I was very angry when I heard their cry and these words.
>
> Then I consulted with myself, and I rebuked the nobles and the rulers, and said unto them: "Ye exact usury, every one of his brother." And I set a great assembly against them. (Neh 5:3–7)

Practically, Nehemiah decreed that all non-commercial debts were to be forgiven and maximum interest rates were set. At the same time he managed to locate, revise, and reissue much older Jewish laws, now preserved in Exodus, Deuteronomy, and Leviticus, that in certain ways went even further. He institutionalized the Law of Jubilee: a law that stipulated that all debts would be automatically cancelled "in the Sabbath year" (that is, after seven years had passed), and that all who languished in bondage because of such debts would be released (Deut 15:1–3; Lev 25:9).

It is no wonder, then, that the concept of "freedom" in the Bible, as in Mesopotamia, came to refer above all to release from the effects of debt. Over time, the history of the Jewish people itself came to be interpreted in this light: so the liberation from bondage in Egypt was seen as God's first paradigmatic act of "redemption." As a religious concept fundamental to Christian theology, it still implies monetary debts being "redeemed," that is, paid off. It is hardly surprising, says Graeber, that this very real liberation from an intolerable burden was adopted by Christians as a psychological category for release from one's burden of sin and guilt.

If so, Graeber continues, redemption is no longer about buying something back. It's more a matter of cancelling that entire system of accounting. In many Middle Eastern cities this was literally true: one of the common acts during debt cancellation was the ceremonial destruction of the tablets on which financial records had been kept; an act against officialdom to be repeated in just about every major peasant revolt in history. Meantime, before any final "redemption," what can be done?

In one of his more disturbing parables, that of the Unforgiving Servant, Jesus deals explicitly with the problem:

> Therefore, the kingdom of heaven is like a king who wanted to settle accounts with his servants. As he began the settlement, a man who owed him ten thousand talents was brought before him. Since he was not able to pay, the master ordered that he and his wife and his children and all that he had be sold to repay the debt.

The servant fell on his knees before him: "Be patient with me," he begged, "and I will pay back everything." The servant's master took pity on him, cancelled the debt, and let him go.

But when that servant went out, he found one of his fellow servants who owed him a hundred denarii. He grabbed him and began to choke him. "Pay back what you owe me!" "Be patient with me, and I will pay you back!"

But he refused. Instead, he went off and had the man thrown into prison until he could pay the debt. When the other servants saw what had happened they were greatly distressed and went and told their master everything that had happened.

Then the master called the servant in. "You wicked servant!" he said, "I cancelled all that debt of yours because you begged me to. Shouldn't you have had mercy on your fellow servant just as I had on you?" In anger his master turned him over to the jailers to be tortured, until he should pay back all he owed. (Matt 18:23–34)

This parable, says Graeber, has long been a challenge to theologians who normally interpret it as a comment on the endless bounty of God's grace and how little he demands of us in comparison. What is even more striking, he comments, is the tacit suggestion that forgiveness, in this world, is ultimately impossible. Christians practically say as much every time they say the Lord's Prayer and ask God to "forgive us our debts, as we also forgive our debtors." As this is not something we normally do, why then should God forgive us our sins?[4]

As I was working on this chapter, I came across an account of a tragic incident in the northern city of Haifa in Israel.[5] Moshe Silman, 57, a son of Holocaust survivors, took a bus from Haifa to Tel Aviv where a social justice protest was to be held. He had a bottle of petrol in his hand. Just as the demo was about to end, he doused himself and lit a match. At the time this was reported, he was in a critical condition with third-degree burns covering 94 percent of his body.

Just before setting himself alight, Silman handed out a letter telling how a small debt of around US $1,000 to the National Insurance Institute had spiraled out of control. He owned a small truck delivery business. His battle against Israeli authorities took him through bankruptcy, mental despair, and eventually severe deterioration in health. He suffered a stroke, could not work, and when he asked for minimum assistance with rent he was turned down. The reporter, Ami Kaufman, noted that Israel's Prime Minister, Binjamin Netanyahu, used an interesting choice of words in his response, calling

4. Ibid., 81–84.
5. *The Guardian*, 19 September 2012.

it a "personal tragedy," as if it had nothing to do with the social structure of the State and did not reflect a much larger disease in society. Two days later, Silman died.

Going back to Graeber, he remarks that Jesus's parable leaves us with the lingering suspicion that we couldn't live up to his standards, even if we tried. World religions are full of this kind of ambivalence. Yet for most of history, what monetary debt has meant to the majority of people is the terrifying prospect of sons and daughters being carried off and being subject to every conceivable form of violence and abuse: the equivalent to being "turned over to the jailers to be tortured." And that's just from the perspective of the father. One can only imagine how it might have felt to be the daughter. Yet, over the course of centuries, millions of fathers and daughters have known (and in fact many, like Moshe Silman, still know) exactly what it's like.[6]

Aristotle condemned this "breeding" of money (that is, money being assumed to have and being used as if it has the regenerative power to create more money) on the grounds that it was most "unnatural." The seventeenth-century Quaker John Bellars noted that money "birthed" from money had become divorced from anything tangible, natural or earthly. And as this happened, it had also become "the measure and scale by which we value all other things"; that is, all living, earthly things. In fact, it is the scale and measure by which we *devalue* them. Taking a sheep as his example, Bellars pointed out that giving it a notional monetary value meant that it lost its implicit value as a living creature—as did the sons and daughters of debtors. That was no longer the basis on which we measure what is valuable to us. Instead, by superimposing a monetary value on an individual creature's life we had devalued what it is in itself. Furthermore, this devaluation was arithmetically progressive. So its intrinsic natural value decreased in proportion to an increase in its monetary value.[7] It was no longer a breeding sheep but a breeder of money.

This monetary, hierarchical devaluation of what Earth and Earth's creatures are in themselves has influenced our thinking and behavior to such an extent that it is now commonly accepted not only that money breeds money, but also that no natural form of life or earthly substance is needed to guarantee its ability to increase in value. Nationally and globally, not even printed paper is needed. In Britain, since the Bank Charter Act of 1844 didn't anticipate the advent of computer-screen credit, less than 3 percent of "money" is backed with actual cash from the Bank of England. The other 97 percent is created electronically by other banks. With computerized technology they are now able to turn a customer's desire for a loan into a "virtual/actual" loan without

6. Graeber, *Debt*, 86.
7. Clarke, *John Bellars*, 98.

having to either "hold" or "print" the equivalent money. The customer's account is similarly debited on-screen at the going interest rate. But both the money and the notional increase now exist only as records on the bank's computer:

> It is this type of money that now makes up 97.4% of all the money used in the British economy. . . . The money created by banks is referred to as commercial bank money. . . . . We might object that the commercial banks are not really creating money—they are extending credit and this is not the same thing.
>
> The Bank (Bank of England) supplies base money on demand at its prevailing interest rate, and "broad" money is created by the banking system. . . . When banks make loans they create additional deposits for those that have borrowed.[8]

This power to "create" money implies the power to generate and regenerate its life: in this instance, through the mental category or concept known as "the life of the economy." Originally based on stamping pieces of metal with uniform designations guaranteeing weight and fineness, governments had to get involved as guarantors. The metallic integrity of coins played a crucial role in the very idea that there was something called "the economy" which operated by its own rules, separate from those of moral or political life. It was and is sustained by our natural propensity to truck and barter.[9] In the previous chapter we saw how Locke and Newton considered false coinage so great a danger to the economy as to impose the death penalty on those found guilty of it. Endangering "the life of the economy" called for drastic counter measures.

But the impulse to increase money not only tends to increase the appropriation of land or property. It also appropriates to itself the "futures" of people, livestock and crops. Their breeding potential is represented as a presumptive future increase in income. This orientation towards the future brings together that hoped-for monetary "increase" with the human desire to generate life or, as Aristotle noted, eternal life. The closest we come to it is continuing one's self through posterity. With interest "generating" wealth, physical inheritance and interest are seen as means of extending identity into quasi-immortality. Over time, their functions have been coordinated into making it socially acceptable to "foster" one's legacy through acquisition of "shares" in future monetary profits. One effect of this has been the development of a culture in which a supposedly unbounded accumulation of quasi-eternal entities takes on an irreversible direction toward an increasing disproportion of possessions.

8. Ryan-Collins, *Where Does Money Come From?*, 16–17.
9. Graeber, *Debt*, 27–28.

The historic role played in this by the process of colonization is now evident in the general acceptance of the continuing appropriation of other peoples' lands and property worldwide, leading to a consequent increase in monetized commercial farming catering for world markets. The colonizers and proprietors of imperial British or Spanish sugar, tea, cocoa, and cotton plantations may no longer be names on supermarket shelves; but the wealth that they accumulated for their heirs—through slave labor—purchased and maintained vast estates, passed on from one generation to the next, and on to the corporate bodies of today. The original personal link between growth and inheritance, between colonizers, their descendants, lands, crops and workers may have disappeared. But it has been replaced by computerized corporate transactions between investors who buy shares in "Africa" that are connected to it only through the mental category of "earning interest." In this context, the "power of money" drives this notional growth in the life of the world economy. At the same time it not only devalues but also steals and despoils the inherited natural resources of indigenous peoples and other-than-human creatures. They are simply absent from computer calculations done at a distance by a relatively small number of human beings. The latter, on behalf of invisible shareholders, make metaphorical but eventually real "killings" through manipulating the money markets.

> Besides interest, and in combination with it, there is another central issue—speculation. The end of currency regulation in 1973 led to an incredible degree of speculation in foreign exchange. As we know, daily foreign exchange transactions, worth about US $1.5 trillion, are over 95% speculative in nature.[10]

Our implicit assent to this subordination of earthly value to human "interest" makes us complicit in its lethal effects on Earth's resource base and biodiverse life forms. There is a parallelism between acceptance of the mental category of interest as the standard of value and the devaluing of natural life. Money has become "a sign with no earthly referent"—other than itself. Bellars saw this happening when money generated by selling a sheep generated twenty times more money than did a similar sheep sold earlier. This "breeding of money" was not paralleled by a comparable increase in sheep numbers. That is why after twenty years, *measured on a monetary scale*, the value of one sheep rose by twenty per cent. The increase was based on the increased monetary return the sale generated, imbuing the money with false reproductive life. The living sheep had become a pawn in the monetary game, its "value" measured solely by price. This implicitly ignored its intrinsic, natural worth. And what was

10. Duchrow and Hinkelammert, *Property for People, Not for Profit*, 193.

true for a sheep applied equally to all other earthly bodies, including those humans sold and bought in slavery.

This devaluing of what is natural, earthy, and intrinsically perishable depended on the positing of the analogies between money and natural forms of breeding condemned as false by Aristotle. Locke was aware of this condemnation, presenting the case for money as counterintuitive by noting that "Land produces naturally something new and profitable and of Value to Mankind," whereas "Money is a barren thing, and produces nothing." Nevertheless, when arguing for rates of interest compared with rent he used the mental category of barrenness to imply its opposite, fruitfulness. These rates are required, he said,

> because of the many, and sometimes long intervals of barrenness, which happen to money more than Land. Money at Use, when returned into the hands of the owner, usually lies dead there, till he gets a new Tenant for it, and can put it out again; and all this time it produces nothing.[11]

In order to remain consistent, remarks Valenze, Locke might have corroborated the conclusions drawn from Aristotle and Aquinas's sense of money as a medium without life. Yet in spite of his awareness of this, he used the *notion* of money as "working capital" that "*earns*" interest through the *notional* activity in which it engages. In another instance, he reached for a nutritional analogy similar to those used by William Petty and Thomas Hobbes:

> For Money being an universal Commodity, and as necessary to Trade, as Food is to Life, everybody must have it, at what Rate they can get it.[12]

The use of mental categories implying money's ability to "work" at increasing its value or to "nourish" people's lives should have been exposed in all its falsity when Richard Nixon announced in 1971 that the U.S. dollar would no longer be redeemable in gold. This marked the beginning of the present phase of "virtual money."[13] Precious metals at least gave some substance, some "body" to the notion of increase by our being able to add to their bodily weight. Indeed, as noted before, the integrity of that weight was seen as so important for the common good that "devaluing" it by "clipping" and so reducing its substantial weight could incur the death penalty. On that basis Locke argued for it as an essential "commodity," as necessary for trade and social cohesion as food is for life.

11. Valenze, *The Social Life of Money*, 61.
12. Ibid.
13. Graeber, *Debt*, 214.

We continue to use such analogies, saying that money "talks" or "circulates" or "lies inactive in accounts"; attributing it with the power to move and generate by talking about "futures" and "derivatives." The mental category of "money breeding money" remains unshattered; though now based on nothing other than tacit human assent or a nebulous faith.

Up to now, however, it has not gone completely unchallenged. Bellars insisted:

> Land, Stock upon it, Buildings, Manifactures, and Mony, are the Body of our Riches; and of all these, Mony is of the least use, until it is parted with. Land and Live Stock increase by keeping, Buildings and Manufactures are useful while kept, but Mony neither increaseth nor is useful, but when it is parted with . . . for as Mony increaseth in quantity, it decreaseth in Value in a Country, except the People and Stock increase in proportion to the Mony.[14]

In agreement with Bellars's common sense view and its syncretism of popular and religious belief, the negative attributes of money also manifested themselves in the evolving image of Mammon. This was made familiar to English culture through the Bible and major works of literature such as *Piers Plowman*, Spenser's *Faerie Queene*, and Milton's *Paradise Lost*. Ancient Aramaic and Hebrew meanings of the word were eclipsed by a specific personification drawn from the King James Version of the New Testament:

> No man can serve two masters; for either he will hate the one, and love the other; or else he will hold to the one, and despise the other. Ye cannot serve God and Mammon. (Matt 6:24)

"Mammon" is actually a transcription of the Aramaic *mamona*. Its roots point to piling up external things that become the definition of one's life.[15] Personalizing this image, religious teachings of the Middle Ages imagined Mammon as a devil endowed with power and dominion, whose association with the underworld converged neatly with his link with the earthly origins of precious metals and added further invidious detail to his identity. The Faustian legend also provided a popular framework for demonic intrusions into daily life where bargains were struck and souls were sold. So the increasing presence and effects of monetary transactions underscored money's involvement with a sinful underworld. English literary accounts like that of Edmund Spenser depicted Mammon mired in earthly concerns, a repulsive creature covered with boughs and shrubs that hide him from "heaven's light."[16]

14. Clarke, *John Bellars*, 98.
15. Douglas-Klotz, *The Hidden Gospel*, 146.
16. Valenze, *The Social Life of Money*, 95.

These Christian images of a three-tiered universe with Earth at its center implicitly devalue Earth in favor of heaven by presenting its "bowels" as the dwelling place of the Demon-God Mammon. He is in charge of riches, renown, honor, estate, and "all this worldes good." In *Paradise Lost* Milton made a similar association between heaps of money, stigmatized activities, and obscure earthly depths, with Mammon directing men to plunder the globe in search of riches. Avaricious agents with impious hands

> Rifled the bowels of their mother Earth
> For treasures better hid. Soon had his crew
> Opened into the hill a spacious wound,
> And digged out ribs of gold. Let none admire
> That riches grow in Hell: that soil may best
> Deserve the precious bane![17]

Milton's contemporaries might have seen a connection between this allusion to gold-mining and the pillaging of precious metals from India, Africa, and South America. Religiously, it held to and reinforced the belief that "Hell" was synonymous with Earth's bowels, as far removed as possible from "Heaven above" and therefore separated from God. John Bunyan registered like sentiments about the gravitational pull of money in *The Pilgrim's Progress*, in which characters like Christian and Mr. Money-love embodied the tension between the ethereal abstraction of heavenly ideals and the profane nature of material reality. When the pilgrims encounter a silver mine, Christian recognizes precious metal as "a snare to those that seek it." He implies the enslaving power of money and underscores the justice of their fate when they, along with Demas the son of Judas, are swallowed up by the earth:

> One calls, the other runs, that he may be
> A sharer in his lucre: so these two
> Take up in this world, and no further go.[18]

The earthly aspect of money, remarks Valenze, ever present and poisonous, threatened to anchor its victim in the world forever: a "hell" firmly situated in Earth and therefore as far as possible from "heaven" and God. But just as paradigms of providence and evidence of divine disfavor were in flux in the seventeenth century, so too were the formal boundaries of money under negotiation. Institutions of church and state realigned their respective roles in the case of usury. Conflicts about its practice diminished after legislation passed in 1571 and particularly after 1624, when the practice of lending with interest

17. Milton, *Paradise Lost*, Book 1.

18. Bunyan, *Pilgrim's Progress*, Part 1, the Seventh Stage.

was no longer seen as a matter within religious jurisdiction: on the grounds that lending at interest benefited society at large. With its economic benefits clearly laid out, the practice of lending was thus defined in technical terms, so that abuses became a matter of individual conscience outside the jurisdiction of the state. In a study of early modern business practices, Richard Grassby summed it up succinctly: "The logic of the market confounded all theology."[19]

So much for Nehemiah's condemnation and Jesus's parable. In their cultural settings, of course, God was the implied just ruler or Father. One greater than the market or even the state: one susceptible to moral arguments and powerful enough to impose justice on those oppressing the indebted. Also, for many seventeenth-century Christians, money was infused with social life and confronted its users with repeated tests of moral probity and charitable awareness, reminding them of choices involving their own desires and the needs of others. For the devout and aptly named Puritan, Nehemiah Wallington, money belonged to a bounded, problematic universe crowded with circulating signs of providence which, like the coins in his cash box, continuously ebbed and flowed, subject to powers outside their own authority. Under the management of divinity, money accreted positive meaning, representing much more than simply income, "for the love of money is the roote of all evil which while some lusteth after they erred from the faith and pearced themselves through with many sorrows."[20]

The power of money, in Wallington's view, could be measured in various magnitudes of physical force in the form of bodily comforts; which in turn desensitized the believer against salutary pricks of conscience. Though clearly he possessed little of it, the comings and goings of money prompted him to contemplate the place of riches and charity in a larger sense; money often represented the part for the whole in the society around him. He saw himself as within a godly commonwealth, as a steward that has nothing but what we have received as we come naked into the world. And when we "return" to where we came from, we must give an account to God of our stewardship. Thus, management of money earned through hard work was part of a common stock, devolving upon an individual in much the same way as a long-term loan, intended to affect justice in the larger social sphere.[21]

He was not alone, says Valenze, in his uncertain search for the right road in business behavior. Quakers such as John Bellars were perhaps the boldest opponents of the customary haggling over prices. What is clear is that in seventeenth-century England, money was firmly situated at the intersection of

19. Valenze, *The Social Life of Money*, 96–97.

20. Ibid., 99–100.

21. Ibid., 101–5.

conflicts between self and other, good and evil, acquisition of money and the effects of its material loss. In other words, its social moral value. What is also clear is that the religious moral basis for that value, God's gift of the land to all who inhabit it, had been subsumed, most effectively by Locke, into a system where, with the use of money, the industrious rational agent has the right to accumulate an unlimited supply of land and so make invalid the natural limits of the state of nature.[22]

The authors of Deuteronomy constantly reminded the Jews that as they had all been slaves in Egypt, had they not all been redeemed by God? Was it right, when they had all been given this Promised Land to share, for some to take that land away from others? Was it right for a population of liberated slaves to go about enslaving one another's children through debt? Analogous arguments were being made in similar situations almost everywhere in the ancient world: in Athens, in Rome, and in China, where legend has it that coinage itself was first invented by an ancient emperor to redeem the children of families who had been forced to sell them after a series of devastating floods.[23]

This kind of monetary exchange is now, thankfully, as redundant as it is inspiring. Yet it still illustrates the very different impacts and possible outcomes of our rootedness in and dependence on environmental resources, as well as our differing ability to use them for our own or others' advantage. The poor remain literally dependent on the goodwill of the rich for their safe access to those resources. Which can devalue them not only in their own eyes but, by their very dependence on them, in the eyes of the rich. When we attempt to understand the impact of environmental changes on human happiness, says, Eric Lambin, we find two recurrent themes: the separation between rich and poor countries and, in the rich countries, the separation between human beings and nature.[24] Valuing Earth as "property" has led to its marketization and to its being viewed almost exclusively in terms of ownership: influencing the lives and environments of both rich and poor. In effect, "property values" have devalued the intrinsic value of our shared planetary resource base that is the primary source of our true well-being.

22. Duchrow and Hinkelammert, *Property for People, Not for Profit*, 63.
23. Graeber, *Debt*, 87.
24. Lambin, *An Ecology of Happiness*, 10.

9

Marketized Earth

A debate about the moral limits of markets would enable us to decide, as a society, where markets serve the public good and where they don't belong. It would also invigorate our politics, by welcoming competing notions of the good life into the public square. . . . It would be folly to expect that a morally more robust public discourse, even at its best, would lead to an agreement on every contested issue. But it would make for a healthier public life. And it would make us more aware of the price we pay for living in a society where everything is up for sale.[1]

Now when we talk about the morality of markets, Wall Street Banks and their reckless misdeeds come to mind, together with hedge funds and bailouts and regulatory reforms. But, says Michael Sandel, the moral and political challenge they pose is more pervasive and more mundane—to rethink the role and reach of markets in our social practices, human relationships and everyday lives. This would make us more aware of the price we pay for living in a society where everything is up for sale—at a profit. Yet the most recent studies on happiness, whether in economics, psychology, or sociology, suggest that beyond a threshold of basic material comfort, money does not buy well-being

1. Sandel, *What Money Can't Buy*, 14–15.

88

or happiness. The relationship over time between the happiness of individuals and their income is weak.[2]

Reading this reminded me of a folk tale I heard as a child. A king was very ill, and his doctors could find neither cause nor cure for the illness. They summoned a wise woman to find out what he needed. "Dress him in the shirt of a happy man!" she ordered. The king's servants went far and wide asking every man they met if he was happy. None would admit to it. Then, on the other side of a wall, they heard a man breaking stones and singing to himself. They leaned over and asked: "Are you happy?" "Sure I'm happy," he replied with a grin. "Will you lend us your shirt?" they asked. "I would," he said, "if I had one!"

A more contemporary example comes from a Gallup poll that, over a period of forty years, asked a large sample of Americans what income was needed for a family of four to live comfortably. Year after year most people calculated an amount that increased as rapidly as their true income. This "hedonic adaptation" showed that the level of well-being remained unchanged or increased only temporarily after new goods were acquired. It was also affected by social comparisons: the pleasure we derive from our material possessions depends in part on the amount of the same goods that others possess. To be among the richest in one's reference group may be more important than achieving a certain income. But once a threshold of prosperity has been crossed, money and material goods contribute little to happiness.[3]

So the pursuit of ever-increasing monetary gain not only fails to increase our happiness. It also "demoralizes" any possible debate about the natural limits of the market by our continual driving them beyond present limits. In doing so, we not only ignore how this fails to achieve more happiness for ourselves: we also ignore what it does to the planet's resource base and to the poorest among us, especially those in wealthy nations. Chris Hedges documents and illustrates the effects on them of our *not* challenging the belief that human beings and human societies should be ruled by the demands of the marketplace. This rule is based, he says, on the belief that we (or rather some of us) have a divine right to Earth's resources and land. Not only that but—as became clear in the chapter on colonization—that some of us also claim to have a divine entitlement to displace and even kill others—human and other-than-human—in order to acquire increasing amounts of personal, corporate, or national wealth from their land.

2. Lambin, *An Ecology of Happiness*, 12–13.
3. Ibid., 15.

This "disease of empire" has, he says, left in its wake a trail of ravaged landscapes and incalculable human suffering, in America as well as across the planet:

> The ruthless hunt for profit creates a world where everything and everyone is expendable. Nothing is sacred. It has blighted inner cities, turned the majestic Appalachian Mountains into a blasted moonscape of poisoned water, soil and air. It has forced workers into a downward spiral of falling wages and mounting debt until laborers in agricultural fields and sweatshops work in conditions that replicate slavery.[4]

Echoing Graeber's historical analysis of debt, Hedges gives a voice to those American communities immediately affected by this ruthless hunt for profit. At the same time, he links their human plight to its simultaneous effects on the soil, water, and air of their environment. In line too with the discussion of "futures" in the preceding chapter, he focuses on the world commodities index as the underlying factor. The most heavily traded index is run by the financial firm Goldman Sachs, which "hoards" futures of rice, wheat, corn, sugar, and livestock, jacking up commodity prices by as much as two hundred percent on the global market. This means, of course, that poor families can no longer afford basic staples and hundreds of millions of poor families in Africa, Asia, the Middle East, and the Americas do not have enough to eat—even as their toil feeds this ever-increasing mania for monetary profit. The technical jargon and cold neutral terminology of "interest rates" and "futures trading" not only mask the reality of what is happening to the land, its inhabitants, and our shared planetary resources. It also, he says, makes the systems operate with a ruthless efficiency.[5]

For those of us who appear not to be immediately damaged by the environmental effects of a global market in commodities, its "technical jargon and coldly neutral terms" effectively demoralize us by undermining our desire or ability to judge its effects, or to examine how they have affected and determined our actual relationship to Earth. And even if we do perceive this and express views contrary to these systems in everyday moral or emotive terms (such as "good," "healthy," "toxic," or "bad"), such attempts, if not simply ignored, are routinely dismissed as "out of date," "sentimental," "uninformed," or "biased"—though the latter charge surely applies more accurately to the technical language of the markets. As Teilhard de Chardin saw, the coercive

---

4. Hedges, *Days of Destruction, Days of Revolt*, xi–xii.
5. Ibid., 268.

power of such mental categories must be shattered if we are to perceive the ineluctable truth of our inescapable relationship with Earth's "mighty matter."

In the case of market jargon it is clear (or rather, it is deliberately obscured) that what a "future" financial gain means for one person actually means a future of untold suffering and loss of life for many people and for countless other living creatures. Hedges's incisive and insightful exploration of the effects of such trading on our ability to empathize with those directly and indirectly affected by it shows that such ability depends on awareness and acceptance of our real and fundamental relationship with Earth: as a shared life resource base for ourselves and all other-than-human creatures.

That understanding of our interdependence is what has been effectively demoralized by a marketized economy in favor of a putative rise in income for the few. It means that we not only need, as Michael Sandel says, to rethink the role and reach of markets in our social practices, human relationships, and everyday lives. We also need a communal morality: that is, an agreed set of behavioral norms that appreciates and safeguards earthly goods and planetary resources held in common. Human activities need to be assessed in terms of their effects on those resources, and of what they mean for the well-being and shared future of the wider Earth community.[6]

Some reasons for the loss of this moral sense in relation to the Earth, its creatures, and our own earthiness emerged in previous chapters, especially the role played by imperial, philosophical, and religious European institutions that continue to influence our lives and self-image today. But not all of the loss of this moral sense can be laid at the door of history. In the latter stages of the Roman Empire over 60 percent of the wealth was gathered at harvest time by a labor force that amounted to over 80 percent of the overall population. "Harvest shocks" caused by unforeseen shortfalls in the crops were the norm and yields varied from year to year. Not surprisingly, therefore, wealth was thought of as lying in the hands of the gods. In 311 CE one of the last pagan emperors, the eastern emperor Maximin Daia, informed the citizens of Tyre that his persecution of the Christians had pleased the gods. The weather had changed for the better.

Christians also took no chances. Like everybody else, they called in ritual experts with a reputation for success in such matters. The rabbis of Palestine too knew what was at stake, pointing out that the great prayers of the Jewish New Year were made for dew and rain: "So that, finally, the members of God's people should not come to depend upon each other like slaves." For everyone, the harvest was a time of final reckoning. The piles of grain gathered on the threshing floor were all that there was.

6. Lambin, *An Ecology of Happiness*, 15.

Yet only a small portion of these piles remained in the hands of the farmers. For each January, the emperor decided the tax budget of the year. Copies of this document, stating the liability of each province, would then be passed down to every city within a province. Members of every town council were held responsible for raising a given sum from within the territory of their city:

> Vested with imperial authority the town councillors descended on the villages and farmsteads within the territories of their cities. Then they came again, not as collectors of taxes but as landowners calling in their rents. . . . It is usually calculated that, with rent and taxes deducted, the farmers would have to face the coming year with under one-third of the harvest on which they has labored. A peasant family could live on such amounts.[7]

The main difference between then and now is an awareness that the empire's prosperity and that of its citizens directly depended on Earth's fruitfulness. And that that fruitfulness depended on more than human labor. "A good harvest was the smile of God or of the gods spreading across an obedient landscape."[8] In the Pergamon Frieze that fruitfulness was made subject to Athena/Roma, endorsing its importance for the survival of the empire as well as acknowledging that Gaia/Earth lay under divine control. In the late seventeenth century, this was religiously and legally ratified by John Locke's social contract theory which visualized a society where authority over the Earth, its lands, resources, and all its other-than-human creatures was given to Man by God. True, that presumed divine mandate was to be maintained either by the assent of the governed or imposed by force. Nevertheless, this ecological religious humility recognized that a greater power than the human is at work in annually maintaining and renewing Earth's resources.

Nowadays, the governance of Earth resources through global financial monetary systems is simply accepted as a "given" by Western governments, that is, given up to the pursuit of monetary profit. The lack of any discussion about the way in which we exercise such a presumed "mandate"—or whether we have a right to claim it—is the hallmark of a morally bankrupt society, one in which, as envisioned by most western governments, everything on Earth is taken to have only market value that is to be maximized at any cost to the natural environment. Correlative to that, Earth's intrinsic value, what it is in itself rather than what monetary value it commands on the stock market, is socially and culturally ignored. Or disdained and dismissed in favor of an increased market value whose reality is solely defined by the algorithms in

7. Browne, *The Secular Ark*, 12–13.
8. Ibid., 12.

the computing machines of financial services. This dominant mindset is fundamental to the present impasse in meeting the challenges of global climate change. And in the continuous depletion and wastage of our shared planetary resources in order to accumulate money.

At the heart of what have become cultural norms is an ancient and pervasive perception of us as a unique species: unique because of our particular relationship to what, in the *Timaeus*, Plato calls "the Father of the universe." The core understanding of this relationship is that this "Father" gives us and us alone, an "immortal soul" or a unique intellect. This view of ourselves influenced later biblical interpretations of the Genesis narrative in which God created a "groundling" or "earthling" in his own image, giving him "dominion" over every living thing (Gen 1:26). Then God breathed into his nostrils the breath of life and he "became a living being" (Gen 2:7). The usual English translation of this last text asserts that he became "a living soul," with "soul" (or "intellect") distinguishing us (supposedly) from all other evolved species.

This claim to uniqueness for our species, with or without its philosophical or religious bases (and certainly without a geological or evolutionary scientific one) still remains a dominant feature of common presuppositions about what it means to be human. The fallacy underlying it is decisively exposed by Mary Midgley in her paper "On Being an Anthrozoon," given to the International Society for Anthrozoology in July 2012.[9] This term, a compound of *anthropos* and *zoon*, emphasizes the fact that humans are animals. As no human has ever been anything *but* an animal, she says, it seems odd that we should now find it hard to grasp this concept. No doubt the claim to our uniqueness is partly to establish our right to exploit other creatures because we see ourselves as entities of a different kind. But, she remarks, the basis for this self-understanding lost credibility when Darwin's work on evolution rejected this hierarchical picture in favor of seeing ourselves as evolving creatures sharing the Earth on equal terms.

This more accurate and informed view of ourselves invites us to serve the interests of *all* life on Earth. For we are slowly learning that only by doing so do we ultimately serve our own. The indissoluble link between our well-being and that of all other living beings, grounded in a shared dependence on Earth's resources, is scientifically beyond doubt. Its truth becomes increasingly evident as individual and collective human decisions to act primarily, or even solely in what appears to be our own interests—such as the destruction of mountaintops, rainforests, and the pollution of fresh water resources—are seen to have taken Earth and ourselves into what economic theorists describe as a state of "moral hazard." The particular understanding of the working

9. Midgley, "On Being an Anthrozoon."

relationships that underlies this term should be noted. Here "moral" means the *customary* human tendency to take undue risks where the costs are not borne by the party taking the risks and profiting from them. On reflection, this reveals an extremely *immoral* tendency in an individual or institution for taking risks whose costs are borne by others. In practice this enables them to act less carefully than they otherwise would because it ensures that they do not suffer the full consequences of their actions. A case in point is the development and use of certain pesticides in farming that are known to be a real and present danger to the life of the honeybee. And with that, to the pollination of other fruit-bearing plants and trees.

Economists describe "moral hazard" as a special case of "information asymmetry," a situation in which the dominant party in a transaction has more information about its actions and intentions than the party that unwittingly pays for any negative consequences of the risks taken by the dominant one. Like all analogies, this can only be taken so far. We signed no exclusive contract for services with Earth, or Earth with us. And our "dominance" over Earth is a cultural and religious delusion. Nevertheless, the analogy throws some light, I believe, on what it *appears* to mean to live in an age dominated by the tenets of global market capitalism. It means relating to Earth solely as a source of monetary profit, whatever the risk to its long-term, shared resource base. And doing so not to meet our needs but to serve our greed for monetary wealth and property.

Pursuing this moral delusion has created highly destructive "market forces" that are apparently so autonomous as to wield more power over us than any democratic institution. As they increasingly dictate our relationship with Earth, so we increasingly ignore our primary obligation of identifying with all members of its life community in our shared dependence on Earth's resources. At the same time, basic moral and religious tenets about protecting the soil from overuse and all the inhabitants of the land from want (cf. Leviticus 25) are now supported by irrefutable evidence that neglecting to do so is not in our own best interests either.

Indeed the morally hazardous enterprise of taking whatever we can from the Earth to serve market forces acts directly against those interests. Yet this enterprise has been and is politically, commercially, and legally encouraged— indeed often enforced. Any land, river, or sea "lying idle," that is, without some industrial, commercial, social, cultural, or human community "value" is liable to be seized by whatever political or economic body assumes property rights over it. Its intrinsic value to all species is ignored on the assumption that the accumulation of money through appropriating and exploiting global resources is a human entitlement.

So we now see enormous mounds of waste materials raised in some of the poorest countries in the world. At the same time, in one of the richest, the United States, the landscape is being "pitted" in the pursuit of mineral wealth. Chris Hedges describes how, in mountaintop removal, the layers of mountain in between layers of coal are blasted to smithereens and dumped into valley fills. When rain trickles through this pulverized rock it can more easily dissolve minerals from the dumps, some of which contain heavy metals that are toxic and in high concentration. From the air you can see weirdly-colored pools of water full of these metals so that people in the hollows get foul-smelling, discolored water in their wells. Trees lying like matchsticks on the sides of the peaks are on fire. The rights and health of those who live on the land are meaningless. Also, as the coal ash deposits have heavy concentrations of carcinogens, disease in the coalfields is rampant. This is the "future" of some of the most beautiful and fertile land in the States, and of all its human and other-than-human inhabitants.[10]

While this immoral economic perspective has governed Western cultures almost from their inception, only now are its global effects on the community of life on Earth becoming apparent. One reason for this is that our customary conduct has been judged "immoral" only in relation to our own species—and then only in relation to some of them. For as Hedges makes clear, the plight of the mountaintop communities is in fact an economic continuation of colonial policies. The appropriation of land and consequent devastation of indigenous cultures continues to service a financial economy imposed on them by force. Rectifying its disastrous outcomes calls for discarding the dominant cultural self-perception in which we assume that the Earth, some of its human, and all its other-than-human inhabitants exist only to serve and enrich us monetarily. No wonder it is now considered scientifically correct to talk about the present epoch in Earth history as the Anthropocene.

But this is no badge of honor. It is emblematic of an unfounded, dangerous claim to a unique status among Earth's creatures and a corresponding right to own and to use Earth's resources for monetary gain. Its hubris is evident in God's challenge to Job:

> Where were you when I laid the foundations of the Earth?
> Tell me, if you have understanding.
> Who determined its measurements—surely you know!
> Or who shut in the sea with doors
> When it burst forth from the womb;
> When I made the clouds its garment
> And thick darkness its swaddling band

10. Hedges, *Days of Destruction, Days of Revolt*, 124–29.

And prescribed bounds for it and set bars and doors,
And said, "Thus far shall you go
And no farther,
And here shall your proud waves be stayed?" (Job 38:4–11)

This divine mockery is heard again in a parable attributed to Jesus in which what seems wisdom to us in our attitudes to Earth's material resources, and in our plans for our own and their "futures," are seen as mere foolishness in God's eyes.

> The land of a rich man brought forth plentifully and he thought to himself, "What shall I do, for I have nowhere to store my crops?" And he said, "I will do this: I will pull down my barns and build larger ones; and there I will store all my grain and my goods. And I will say to my soul, "Soul, you have ample goods laid up for many years; take your ease, eat, drink and be merry." But God said to him, "Fool! This night your soul is required of you and the things you have prepared, whose will they be?" (Luke 12:16b–20)

This parable can be heard in a number of different ways: as a midrash on a parable in Ben Sira (11:12–28), or as a piece of folk wisdom found in aphoristic form in many cultures. The range of meanings also includes that of the English colloquialism, "You can't take it with you!" as well as the sardonic comment of Ernest Bramah's Chinese sage, Kai Lung: "He who thinks he is raising a mound may only in reality be digging a pit."[11] Today it can also be heard as an ecological parable intended to shock those of us with ample resources into awareness of what we as a species are doing to those of us who have none—and are doing *a fortiori* to all other species. Laying up ample resources or stockpiling them in anticipation of future market price rises leaves empty pits for those coming after us.

The barns of Jesus's parable can certainly be seen as exemplifying the folly of such short-term policies that take no account of their real "future": that is, of their long-term effects on a community's resource base. But they have an even stronger contemporary resonance. For if the fool represents the human species, then our present reckless accumulation of money through the buying and selling of natural resources means that future generations will have none to inherit. Then Aristotle's insight into the impulse to accumulate wealth as being an investment in posterity, thereby prolonging one's life, acquires a new and somber twist. For God's question can then be heard another way: "Fool! Will there be anyone to inherit these possessions?" To adopt Kai-Lung's vivid

11. Bramah, *Kai Kung's Golden Hours*, 30.

imagery, we are so intent on raising the mound before us that we ignore the empty pit left for those coming after us.

As far as I know, this is the only instance in the canonical Christian scriptures where God (in person, so to speak) is said to address someone as "Fool!" It is, therefore, as definitive a religious moral statement as we are likely to find of the difference between prevailing market attitudes to the future, whatever form they take, and the moral responsibility of being a member of the community of life on Earth. Plans to increase monetary wealth regardless of the cost to Earth may appear "wise" to us. But in taking no account of their effects on our shared future, they are in fact the height of folly.

I thought I had finished writing this chapter. Then came the morning paper, *The Guardian,* and in it a precise and chilling overview by George Monbiot of the present British Government's plans for the national environment. Under the heading "Putting a Price on the Rivers and Rain Diminishes Us All," he describes those plans and their use of an "inspiring new lexicon" in laying out the capitalization and cultural demoralization of British attitudes to the Earth:

> The UK now has a "natural capital committee," an Ecosystem Markets Task Force and an inspiring new lexicon. We don't call it nature any more: the proper term is "natural capital." Natural processes have become "ecosystem services," as they exist only to serve us. Hills, forests and river catchments are now "green infrastructure," while biodiversity and habitats are "asset classes" within an "ecosystem market." All of them will be assigned a price, all of them will become exchangeable. . . . Commodification, economic growth, financial abstractions, corporate power; aren't these the processes driving the world's environmental processes? Now we are told that to save the biosphere we need more of them.[12]

This new lexicon of mental categories such as "natural capital" and "ecosystems services" derives directly from what Max Weber called the "specific and peculiar rationalism of western culture" that is the basis for modern capitalism. But, he said, its development is also determined by the ability and disposition of men to adopt certain types of "practical rational conduct." Here presumably it is engaged in setting up a "natural capital committee" and "an ecosystems Task Force."

Almost a century after Weber's analysis of the language, methodology and implementation of capitalism, the truth of his conclusion is borne out by its effectively demoralizing Earth into the status of "a human asset class."

---

12. Monbiot, "Putting a Price on the Rivers and Rain Diminishes Us All."

And to what does this reduce us?

> In fact, the summum bonum of this ethic, the earning of more and more money, is combined with the strict avoidance of any spontaneous enjoyment of life. . . . Man is dominated by the making of money, by acquisition as the ultimate purpose of his life.[13]

13. Weber, *The Protestant Ethic and the Spirit of Capitalism*, 18.

10

Peaceable Earth

When iron was found, the trees began to tremble, but the iron reassured them: "Let no handle made from you enter into anything made from me, and I shall be powerless to injure you." Genesis Rabba 5.[1]

This story comes from a fourth-century rabbinic commentary on the biblical creation narrative. It was a moment of crisis in the life of a Jewish people facing the reality of a militant Christianity governed and led by the successors of Constantinian Rome. Yet the rabbis did not offer the image of an omnipotent God who would come to save them. Instead, strong in their foundational belief in the creative unity of all life on Earth, they used a natural image to remind us that, as it is our own hands that create the weapons that destroy us, so the decision whether or not to use them is also in our hands.

That advice, given so long ago, seems more distant than ever today when the destructive power of militarism far outweighs any efforts at peace building. In 1992, before the first Earth Summit in Rio of the United Nations Conference on Environment and Development (UNCED), the Latin American churches asked that the problem of militarism be put on the environmental agenda. On being informed that the Conference would only talk about "defense," those churches asked the World Council of Churches to address

---

1. From a selection of quotes online: http://www.sacred-texts.com/jud/tmm/tmm07. htm.

the subject of militarism at its Rio conference held prior to UNCED. I was given that task. It involved spending many uncomfortable, indeed harrowing months researching the topic. More positively, it also meant that I spent time with organizations and individuals devoted to furthering global peace programs and dedicated to highlighting the overwhelming importance of such programs for the life of the whole Earth community.

The most heartfelt and, in many cases, angry and bitter responses at Rio prompted by what I had to say about militarism came from representatives of countries that had been colonized by Christian European nations. During the intervening five hundred years the devastating legacy of those military conquests had shaped and continues to shape their lives and their land: through economic exploitation as well as industrial, agricultural, commercial, and bodily injury in all its forms. The sword of Roma/Athena wielded by Christian colonizers against Gaia/Earth continued to bring death to her and her offspring, human and other-than-human, most devastatingly through continuous trading based on slave labor:

> At every point, the familiar but peculiarly European entanglement of war and commerce reappears—often in startling new forms. The first stock markets in Holland and Britain were based mainly in trading shares of the East and West India companies, which were both military and trading ventures. For a century, one such private, profit-seeking corporation governed India. The national debts of England, France and others were based in money borrowed not to dig canals and erect bridges, but to acquire the gunpowder needed to bombard cities and to construct the camps required for the holding of prisoners and the training of recruits. . . . The Atlantic slave trade can be imagined as a giant chain of debt-obligation stretching from Bristol to Calabar to the headwaters of the Cross River. . . . The middlemen in these chains connected . . . the stock-jobbers in London with Bengali tea plantations or Amazonian rubber-tappers.[2]

Today, internal and external armed conflicts are nourished and sustained by supplies of weapons made by major "defense" industries quoted on the New York and London Stock Exchanges. Leading exporters of them are the United States, Russia, France, China, Germany, the UK, and Italy. The biggest spenders on military hardware are the USA $689bn; China $129bn; Russia $64bn; France $58.2bn; UK $57.9bn (all $ quoted are US).[3] Such vast sums spent on researching and manufacturing weapons of destruction impoverish as well

2. Graeber, *Debt*, 346–47.
3. Online: http://www.sipri.org/databases/milex/.

as endanger the lives of the whole human community. Simultaneously, they implicitly threaten those of all other-than-human creatures as well as the continued health and supply of our shared planetary resources.

David Graeber suspects that we are looking at the final effects of the militarization of American capitalism itself. At its root is a veritable obsession on the part of the rulers of the world—in response to the upheavals of the 1960s and 1970s—to ensure that social movements cannot be seen to grow, flourish, or propose alternatives; and that those who challenge existing power arrangements can never be seen to win. To do this requires a vast apparatus of armies, prisons, police, various forms of private security firms and military intelligence apparatus.

> Maintaining this apparatus seems even more important, to exponents of the "free markets," than maintaining any sort of viable market economy. How else can one explain what happened in the former Soviet Union? One would have imagined that the end of the Cold War would have led to the dismantling of the army and the KGB and rebuilding the factories, but in fact what happened was precisely the other way around.[4]

The global effects are visible too in the militarization of popular culture. At Rio, one African mother raised the question of the military toys and games her children were being given as presents. The sound of gunshots, explosions, and aircraft excites them, she said, giving them what she regarded as the wrong kind of role models and aspirations. Violence is depicted as the ultimate solution to human problems. War-toy sales jumped from an estimated $325 million in 1982 to nearly $1 billion by 1984. I hate to think what the sum is today. Interactive computer games and major films, such as *The Hunger Games*, thrillingly parody and at the same time conceal the real effects of both war and famine. Fashion models parade in military-styled outfits and those involved in leisure pursuits such as hunting, hiking, climbing, and diving use accessories modeled on combat gear. Such formative cultural influences help obscure the fact that militarism, in all its bodily forms, spends vast amounts of resources (not least those of language) concealing the reality that the main purpose and outcome of war is *injuring*: injuring human bodies designated as "enemies." With all such "unintended" damage to civilians and other-than-human bodies trivialized as "collateral damage."

For militarism's language of "defense" hides the reality that what actually happens in war is too horrific and therefore too counterproductive to be openly acknowledged. The physical structures of warfare not only require the

4. Graeber, *Debt*, 382.

injuring of bodies but also that those injured be concealed from view; or, when they do appear, that they are clad in the flags of national victory. The mental categories used for describing the effects of wars are part of a techno-strategic rationality that uses abstractions, redescriptions, and metaphors to obscure the intense and extensive suffering wrought by monstrously destructive weapons. All "played out" in the "theater" of warfare.

It is no aberration that the test site for the atom bomb was dubbed "Trinity," or that a nuclear missile can be called "Peacekeeper." Bloody conflicts are presented in increasingly sophisticated diagrams and computer models that sanitize and distance us from the horrors inflicted through modern armed conflict. Moreover, the speed and funding of technological advance creates an inbuilt obsolescence in weapons manufacture. So Western military powers ensure that they have the newest and most deadly models, creating ever increasing stockpiles of these which, as they become redundant, are then sold relatively cheaply to others engaged elsewhere in combat or indeed in crime.

What jumps out at David Graeber in his work on the history of debt, when comparing Christianity with the Muslim world, are the links in the former between finance, trade, and violence.[5] That violence is now deliberately cloaked by euphemisms such as "soft targets" (unarmed civilians) or "surgical strikes" (air bombings and strafing accurately dosed and targeted). The incidental, "unintentional" killing and poisoning of other-than-human bodies inhabiting and enriching the soil and waters is, as I said, dismissed as "collateral damage." This euphemism is particularly useful today for describing the effects of "drones" on civilian populations. These unmanned aircraft are now routinely used for targeting and destroying enemies where they are safely "embedded" in friendly, neutral or largely civilian territory. A name like "Agent Orange" only lost its ambiguity with the publication of its actual effects: a Vietnamese child on fire running down the road and screaming in agony. Pacific Islanders evicted from their homes because their islands were to be used as testing grounds for atomic weapons were told that the tests were necessary "for the good of mankind and to end all wars." This was after Nagasaki and Hiroshima, where either or both of those abstract premises had been tested beyond all doubt. For it is not abstractions but actual bodies that kill or are killed, drive tanks and staff missile silos are trained to become instruments of "higher purpose."

The abuse of human bodies begins with the education, physical and mental, of the soldiers themselves. I doubt if Plato is required reading in military barracks; but he may well have figured in the education of those who founded them or now run them. For there is a definite connection between

5. Ibid., 291.

his philosophy of education, its influence on Western elite male and clerical educational self-perceptions and the kind of military syllabus envisaged in his writings. As I said in Chapter 3, he formulated a new conceptual type of language that, over time, has helped to replace that fostered and fed by oral narrative with its externalized, "sound and senses" thinking. The change from this to internalized reactions and thought processes produced a psychological, indeed physiological shift in the ratio of the senses used to discover and enact a shared, desensitized self-perception.

This is particularly evident in the dialogues on the education of the guardians in *The Republic,* Book III. There Plato insists on monitoring the types of stories that are told, limiting them to those that give the pupils the least fear of death and indeed lead them to prefer death to defeat. The emphasis on masculinity, reinforced by deriding any show of weakness as feminine, creates the aura of the warrior-hero. His characteristics are a proclivity for violence and an explicit rejection of any show of weakness, physical or intellectual:

> Shouldn't they be told stories that will make them least afraid of death? Or do you think that anyone ever becomes courageous if he's possessed by this fear? . . .
>
> Then we must supervise such stories and those who tell them, and ask them not to disparage the life of Hades in this unconditional way, but rather to praise it, since what they now say is neither true nor beneficial to future warriors. . . .
>
> We'll ask Homer and the other poets not to be angry if we delete these passages. . . . [T]he more poetic they are, the less they should be heard by men who are supposed to be free and to fear slavery more than death. . . .
>
> They may be well and good for other purposes, but we are afraid that our guardians will be made softer and more malleable by such shudders . . .
>
> We'd be right, then, to delete the lamentations of famous men, leaving them to women (and not even to good women either) and to cowardly men, so that those we say we are training to guard our city will disdain to act like that.[6]

The continuity between this thought-world and the military lifeworld of today shows the deliberate shaping of the military mind by abstractions and metaphors that *obscure* the intense and extensive suffering wrought by monstrously destructive and deadly weapons. "Survivability" is a category applied to missiles not life forms, whether human or other-than-human. It now defines the capability to attack targets without military personnel having to face the

6. Cooper, ed., *Plato: Complete Works,* 1022–25.

weaponry of enemy air defenses directly; a goal that has now been achieved by the United States in the development of unmanned missiles. Their "survivability" rests on their ability to reach a "target" undetected (or at least unintercepted) and so ensure that no one targeted, human or other-than-human, survives. The possibility of any feelings of pity, repugnance or remorse for the pain inflicted is excised by reducing the attack to a display of overwhelming, exciting force pictured on a screen.

This latest military endeavor is part of a chain of events that has its origins in the decision by the militant Christian nations of Britain and the United States to invade Iraq in response to the 9/11 attack on New York in 2001. Direct, indirect, and continuing consequences are now seen in Afghanistan, Iraq, and throughout the Middle East. Reaction to them within Western cultures is now based, to a large extent, on their being presented in opposing categories of religious difference. That of "white Christian identity" (claimed by the Norwegian mass murderer Anders Behring Breivik) is opposed, literally and figuratively, to that of "Islamist terrorist" (routinely attached to Osama Bin Laden). No mass murderer represents a community, even if one claims to do so. Yet both have become what they are within the context of social, religious, and economic abstractions which, as Breivik proved to the dismay of his countrymen, appeared to offer him enough support and justification for what he did. Making this religious polarizing of people a basis for violence is the hallmark of a theology of conquest: one historically and most effectively deployed by Christian colonizers.

Yet it has long been claimed as a hallmark of Christianity that the story told of the Messiah, the one anointed in God's name who would bring peace on Earth, came true in Jesus of Nazareth. Those who attend church services throughout the year implicitly assent and indeed loudly proclaim their belief that Jesus the Anointed One, "the Christ," is the Prince of Peace. He is the one who came to establish all-embracing peace, not only within human hearts and among nations, but also in the harmonious living together of all creation when "the lion would lie down with the lamb." The particularity of Jesus's life as Christ-Messiah was and remains a symbol both of continuity and discontinuity with Jewish history. The messianic claims made by Christians about Jesus were based on the eager expectation within post-exilic and later Judaism of what would follow from the coming of the Messiah. This was expressed in the psalmist's poetic description of the ideal king, the one who would "make wars cease to the end of the earth; break the bow, shatter the spear, burn the chariot with fire" (Ps 46:9).

He was personalized in a famous prophetic passage referring to the pagan king, Cyrus, who allowed the Jews to return to Jerusalem from exile:

Behold my servant, whom I uphold,
my chosen, in whom my soul delights;
I have put my spirit upon him,
he will bring forth justice to the nations
He will not cry or lift up his voice
Or make it heard in the street;
A bruised reed he will not break
And a dimly burning wick he will not quench;
he will faithfully bring forth justice.
He will not fail or be discouraged
till he has established justice in the earth;
and the coastlands wait for his law. (Isaiah 42:1–4)

This passage is used by Matthew to identify Jesus (Matt 12:18–21). It is endorsed by Jesus's own words to those who would be his disciples:

Love your enemies and pray for those persecuting you so that you may become sons of your Father; for he raises his sun on bad and good, and rains on the just and unjust. (Matt 5:44–45; Luke 6:27–28, 35)

This expectation of a messianic priest-king who would bring peace to all beings on earth was integral to those readings of the Jewish scriptures that shaped the religious consciousness of the early Christian communities, especially those persecuted by the Roman Emperors. But a different interpretation, in discontinuity with this expectation, gained ground as Christians began to claim that they had experienced God's unique and particular fulfillment of Jewish prophecy in the man Jesus, crucified by Rome. This focused attention on what now apparently divided them from Jews: their spiritual allegiance to a radically different image of the Messiah. That was established at the Council of Nicaea, convened by the Emperor Constantine in the year 312 CE.

The Christian chronicler Eusebius outlined this image when describing the imperial banquet at the conclusion of the Council:

Detachments of the bodyguard and troops surrounded the entrance of the palace with drawn swords, and through the midst of them the men of God (the bishops) proceeded without fear into the innermost of the imperial apartments, in which some were the emperor's companions at table while others reclined on couches arranged on either side. One might have thought that a picture of Christ's kingdom was thus shadowed forth.

Who, asks Dominic Crossan, other than an imperialist Christian, could have thought that this was an image of the messianic banquet foreshadowed in

Jesus's table fellowship with the poor, with women, with the outcast and the sinner?[7] His metaphorical imagery presents God not as a Lord and Emperor to be served in fear but as a compassionate Father: "Be full of pity, just as your Father . . . is full of pity" (Luke 6:36; Matt 5:48).

These opposing images are at the heart of the difference between a militarist Christianity modeled on empire and a peaceable one based on human sharing and participation in the community of earthly life. The first is identified within the early written Christian tradition as *koinon*, the rule of imperial Rome exemplified in Constantinian Christianity. The second, *koinonia*, is the term used in the Acts of the Apostles to describe the peaceful cultivation of unity and the sharing of God's gifts within the first Christian community in Jerusalem and then, by extension, within the larger community of life on Earth. This characterized Jesus's relationships "from below," cultivated in the name of the God who created "all things good" and who cares for them without discrimination.

Where Caesar held the image of divine ruler, he acted as either supreme warlord or peacemaker in order to "impose" order and make peoples "one" in him. In the messianic *koinonia*, unity in the name of the God of Jesus *created* a civic and religious space where, understanding his command to love our enemies, Jesus the Jew could ask a Samaritan woman for a drink and a colonized Jew, Peter, could offer peace and membership of Jesus's community to a colonizing centurion, Cornelius—and have it gratefully accepted.[8]

This last was particularly difficult for the Christian Jerusalem community to accept. For them, Cornelius epitomized the direct opposite of maintaining and cultivating unity on Earth and between all Earth's creatures. *Koinon* was the rule of law based on and expressed in the ability of its Emperor to impose unity and order by force of arms. *Koinonia*, on the other hand, is the ideal of a community living together in a harmony based on Jesus's vision of a universal, non-discriminatory God. The profound differences between them in lifestyle, religious practice, the use of physical force, and the recognition of our unity with all creatures could not be greater. For they symbolize two opposing models of divine power. One, that of imperial power based on military force. The other, the power of peacemaking based on our unity with Jesus within all Earth's creatures.[9]

Paul, a pre-Constantinian Roman citizen, wrote to the Roman community in Ephesus:

7. Crossan, *Jesus*, 96–97.
8. Primavesi, *Cultivating Unity*, 97.
9. Ibid., 26–29.

For he [Christ Jesus] is our peace, who has made us both one, and has broken down the dividing wall of hostility by abolishing in his flesh the law of commandments and ordinances, that he might create in himself one new man in place of the two, so making peace, and might reconcile us both to God in one body through the cross, thereby bringing the hostility to an end. And he came and preached peace to you who were far off and peace to those who were near; for through him we both have access in one Spirit to the Father. (Eph 2:14–18)

Yet here too we see the problem of adapting this vision to the mental categories of the prevailing culture. For Paul remained Roman citizen enough to counsel:

Finally, be strong in the Lord and in the strength of his might. Put on the whole armor of God, that you may be able to stand against the wiles of the devil. For we are not contending against flesh and blood, but against the principalities, against the powers, against the world rulers of this present darkness, against the spiritual hosts of wickedness in the heavenly places.

Therefore take the whole armor of God, that you may be able to withstand in the evil day and having done all, to stand. Stand, therefore, have girded your loins with truth, and having put on the breastplate of righteousness, and having shod your feet with the equipment of the gospel of peace [!]; above all taking the shield of faith, with which you can quench all the flaming darts of the evil one. And take the helmet of salvation and the sword of the Spirit, which is the word of God. (Eph 6:10–17)

What we have here is the language of continuous warfare being "spiritualized" to describe the Christian way of life. Even though first-century Christians, as a persecuted minority, were unlikely, indeed unable to take it literally, the image of the Spirit as a sword, as a weapon to defend oneself against an enemy or hack others to pieces, was already there waiting for Constantinian legitimation and physical form.

Nowadays, while we too live in a militarized culture, our experience is not that of Paul or of a first-century slave faced with the savagery of the Roman army, but of global war involving whole populations and ravaging the Earth. But the pervasiveness of the mental categories of warfare in describing Christian life, supposedly in imitation of Jesus, still functions both as a personal image in devotional literature and as a foundational one in Christian rituals and sermons. This has left us with what the late Walter Wink called "the myth of redemptive violence." Although, he hastens to add, the belief that violence "saves" is so successful because it doesn't seem in the least mythic:

Violence simply appears to be the nature of things. It's what works. It seems inevitable; the last and, often, the first resort in conflicts. If a god is what you turn to when all else fails, violence certainly functions as a god. What people overlook is the religious character of violence. It demands from its devotees an absolute obedience-unto-death. The Myth of Redemptive Violence is the real myth of the modern world. It, and not Judaism or Christianity or Islam, is the dominant religion in our society today.[10]

Emerging awareness of our shared dependence on the Earth's resources offers a direct challenge to this Myth of Redemptive Violence. It calls for non-combative and non-exploitative relationships between ourselves and with other-than-human creatures that resonate with the Messianic vision of Jesus and the earliest Christians—and today with individuals or small religious groups dedicated to nonviolence such as the Quakers. All these try to cultivate unity between us, rather than discriminating against each other on the grounds of creed, gender, race, or species. It is a tragic irony that where the victims of Christian violence have been or are other Christians (as in the intra-Christian wars waged in Europe after the Reformation) it is their opposing claims to represent a Messiah of peace that are trumpeted, even as they inflict torture and death on each other.

So historically, the "triumph" of the "Prince of Peace" has in fact been his defeat. The theological tragedy at the heart of Christianity is that having originated with events that radically challenged the prevailing notion of divine power—the *koinon* of Caesar—by and large it has opted for a theology of re-demptive violence. Its "message" is a rationalization of Christian engagement with coercive forces rather the apostolic *koinonia* of the peaceful, compas-sionate, and nonviolent God of Jesus. This is no longer just a question of re-lationships between religious bodies and their adherence to opposing church doctrines. It puts in question the whole idea of Christianity being "good news" in a world where the ravages of economic and military power, exercised by nominally Christian nations, clearly affect the body of Earth and its whole community of life.

Yet, Christianity claims as its Messiah a man who taught and lived out love of enemies, forgiveness and non-retaliation; who was renowned for heal-ing bodies and attending to their wounds; one who, quoting Isaiah, spoke of the Spirit of God as thirst-quenching water poured out on the thirsty land; a Spirit that would bless their children who would spring up "like grass amid waters" (Isa 44:3–4; John 4:10–14). Confusion about the nature of divine power manifested in Jesus has allowed Christians to claim that the Messiah

10. Wink, "Facing the Myth of Redemptive Violence."

has come while living as though he had not. This doublethink assumes ever greater importance when it is made within the context of the destruction of our shared planetary resources.

Taking the manner of the bodily death of Jesus as an act of violence that has already happened, and believing that the manner of it must be remembered so that it cannot happen again, there is a prophetic voice that says this destruction of the natural world, its diversity of life and global richness, is an act of violence that must not be allowed to happen. Instead, the manner of Jesus's life should lead us to seek to bring justice and peace into being throughout the whole body of Earth. Especially when confronted by a nuclear arms race that, born of our military rationalization and technological mastery in killing living creatures, holds hostage all life on the planet.

Meanwhile, we share the hope expressed so eloquently by Gerald Manley Hopkins:

> When will you ever, Peace, wild wooddove, shy wings shut,
> Your round me roaming end, and under be my boughs?
> When, when, Peace, will you, Peace? I'll not play hypocrite
> To own my heart: I yield you do come sometimes; but
> That piecemeal peace is poor peace. What pure peace allows
> Alarms of wars, the daunting wars, the death of it?
> O surely, reaving Peace, my Lord should leave in lieu
> Some good! And so he does leave Patience exquisite,
> That plumes to Peace thereafter. And when Peace here does house
> He comes with work to do, he does not come to coo,
> He comes to brood and sit.[11]

11. Hopkins, *Poems,* 42.

11

One Earth

*What, then, is this new principle, this force that means revolution? Put
in its briefest form, it is the idea and the challenge of the One. This
challenging idea is firstly the One Thing, the one thing that alone is
needful, that which has been commanded, the good, the right. Secondly
and mainly, it means the one Being who has proclaimed this One Thing
and demands it from us, the One God beside whom there is none else.
And finally, it means the unity and totality of [hu]man[s with all living
beings]. It means that through this One Thing, and therefore with our
whole heart and soul, we are to serve the one God.*[1]

First published in 1931, this unified and revolutionary vision of our lives on
Earth comes from a German Jewish Rabbi, Leo Baeck. He later endured the
horrors of Theresienstadt concentration camp, emerging from it as an elo-
quent embodiment of peacefully meeting "the challenge of the One." For him,
it meant carrying out the command to do what is needful, right, and good,
even in the direst circumstances. The revolutionary force of his deceptively
simple message of oneness not only continues to challenge ideas about our
lives and about the world today. It also challenges us to make the principle
of the "One" a reality by cultivating a unity that already exists. In its simplest

1. Baeck, *God and Man in Judaism*, 23–24.

terms, this requires "One Thing" from us: a living, wholehearted commitment to doing what is good and right among and for all members of the One community of life on Earth. For Baeck, the revolutionary force unifying the world is the belief that through doing what is good and right we serve the One God: and so preserve and enhance the Oneness of life.

For Christians this bond between belief and action is exemplified both in Jesus's life and in the lives of his apostles living in *koinonia* (Acts 2:42). The revolutionary force behind this lifestyle at that time is defined by Richard Pervo as "cultivating unity": that is, serving the God of Jesus rather than the militarist *koinon* of a deified Roman Emperor.[2] Despite the fact that the Roman *koinon* would prevail within European Christianity after the Council of Nicaea (325 CE), the ideal of *koinonia* persisted. It persists today as a challenge to Christians, both individually and as members of official Christian churches. The challenge is met wherever "doing what is right and good" means refusing to differentiate between humans on the grounds of gender, race, or creed, and between ourselves and other-than-human creatures in order to justify violence against them. Wherever the challenge is met and whether or not it is met in Jesus's name, it offers a good and right response to his appeal to live peaceably. He based this on the unity of God's practical and nondiscriminatory concern for all Earth's creatures:

> Love your enemies and pray for those persecuting you so that you may become children of your Father; for he raises his sun on bad and good, and rains on the just and unjust (Matt 5:44–45; Luke 6:27–28, 35).

As a Jew subject in life as in death to military authority, Jesus's appeal to "love your enemies" (which means acting nonviolently toward them) foreshadows that of Leo Baeck by emphasizing that doing what is good and right for all, regardless of their attitude to us personally, is the proper religious response to the One creating and sustaining the life of all. And that living according to this principle is a moral imperative that may make life-changing demands on us; even to death itself. Both Jesus and Baeck responded positively to their Deuteronomic vision of a God "who is not partial and takes no bribes," or in modern terms, "has no favorites" (Deut 10:17). This is a God who sees our earthly lives as a whole; One whose unifying gaze encompasses all creatures within a planet supporting all life from the beginning of time:

> And if you will obey my commandments which I command you this day, to love the Lord your God, and to serve him with all your heart and with all your soul, he will give the rain for your land in

2. Primavesi, *Cultivating Unity*, 17–29.

its season, the early rain and the later rain, that you may gather
in your grain and your wine and your oil. And he shall give grass
in your fields for your cattle, and you shall eat and be full. (Deut
11:13–15)

This Jewish religious premise for living nonviolently, for supporting and being
supported by a peaceable earth community, is now backed by what Bill Ellis
calls the social/scientific Gaian paradigm. Its basic premise is that Gaia/Earth
has evolved and is evolving as a "unit" within and through which we and all
other creatures also evolve.[3] While it is easy to nod our assent to this definition, it is more difficult to act on it. For generally we behave as though there
is an implicit social or scientific mandate that assumes we are independent
of or indeed in charge of the natural world to which we belong. But what we
also have is a unique ability to understand the laws that govern and unify our
world and, based on that understanding, to foster a corresponding rational
desire to live accordingly. That is what both enables and obliges us to cultivate
our oneness by developing and nurturing this idea of ourselves; and living up
to it.

James Lovelock describes his scientific Gaia theory as looking at the
whole Earth from outside (as space exploration has enabled us to do) and
seeing it as a living entity. This involves more than a change of viewpoint as it
belongs within the realm of emergent phenomena where the whole is always
more than the sum of its parts.[4] Our present insights into climate change and
its effects are based on the scientific premise that the sun, the rain, tempera-
ture rises, and droughts ultimately affect friend and foe, cattle and grass, bee
and bear, bird and fish, tree and seed alike. And that now, our lifestyles are
making disproportionate demands on this shared resource base. This premise
serves to reinforce the religious one for living peaceably.

So in practice, continuous monitoring by the Norwegian National Science and Data Centre (NSIDC) of the effects of the melting of the Arctic ice
sheets on the global atmosphere, wild life, biodiversity, plant life, and seas
worldwide not only challenges Northern Atlantic governments to continue
funding such research: it should also challenge them to *discontinue* funding the production of ever more sophisticated and deadly weaponry such as
the nuclear submarines housed in Scotland at Faslane and in France at Ile
Longue, with their warheads supplied and maintained by the United States.
The problem however, in a capitalist culture dominated by militarized world

3. Ellis, *A Gaian Paradigm*, 162.
4. James Lovelock in his foreword to Primavesi, *Sacred Gaia*, xii.

economies, is drawing agreed conclusions from scientific premises that favor both those we think of as friends and those we think of as enemies.

To do this would go against the aims and perceived *koinon* or national interests of governmental and bureaucratic apparatuses that create and maintain massive "defense" and "security" industries. These have been built up within a pervasive climate of fear, jingoistic conformity, and despair of change that renders any thought of a different world order seem idle fantasy. Maintaining, indeed prioritizing them means that ecologically, they are dead weight: army units, guns, surveillance systems, obsolete and developing nuclear weapons as well as propaganda engines, are extraordinarily expensive—and produce nothing.[5] They reflect and recreate the Roman *koinon* of our age: once again Athena's deadly weapons slay Gaia's offspring.

The weapons now are in many different hands, and have even been seen as a necessary response to many environmental developments, seen as both bad and good depending on your point of view. As far back as 1987 Gro Harlem Brundtland, president of the UN Commission on the Environment and Development, asserted:

> Nations have often fought to assert or resist control over war materials, energy supplies, land, river basins, sea passages and other key environmental resources.[6]

Lambin goes on to discuss different aspects of what he calls "environmental security" and "categories of conflict" often linked to degradation of the environment. It lowers agricultural production and increases unemployment, leading to a weakening of rural economies, erosion of traditional social networks, and the migration or displacement of a higher proportion of the population. So ethnic conflicts arise alongside independence movements as well as rebellions, genocides, and guerilla warfare. The trafficking of natural resources extracted illegally and terrorism around mineral mines is accompanied by migration of the young unemployed to the slums of large cities where gangs rule. The tragic reality of all this can be read and seen daily on international media.

Yet globally, by 2006 the number of armed conflicts had diminished by a third. This happened because, faced with a growing scarcity of natural resources, human societies developed possible adaptive responses other than violent conflict by modifying institutions that regulate access to those resources and their use. This was accompanied by a more equitable redistribution of wealth; by technological innovation and the development of an economic sector that consumes fewer resources as well as migration and commercial exchanges

5. Graeber, *Debt*, 382.
6. Lambin, *An Ecology of Happiness*, 108.

with neighboring regions in order to compensate for the scarcity of a local resource. These examples of "cultivating unity" are institutional measures that manage the competition and conflict surrounding natural resources in order to keep them from degenerating into armed violence. It is essential, Lambin says, to distinguish between rare violent conflicts in the struggle for natural resources and nonviolent ones more often resolved by diplomacy and negotiation. This includes negotiation at international level conducted with a degree of constructive effort no other international challenge has ever generated.[7]

As the reference to the NSIDC website makes clear, present scientific technologies and their wide usage also contribute positively to raising awareness of our global interconnectedness and encouraging shared positive responses. They offer unprecedented opportunities for seeing our individual lives as interdependent and sustained by the same earthly resources as all other creatures. In today's global political *koinon*, the life-enhancing scientific conclusions that are and can be drawn from such data-based premises reinforce Baeck's challenge to us to do what is right and good for the unity of life.

But this is not generally made explicit by climate scientists, as I learned at a conference on Johan Rockström's planetary resources model. Nor do they accept that doing so is part of their job description. They present experimental results in scientific categories for judgment by their peers whose task is to examine and to judge the scientific conclusions drawn rather than base moral imperatives on them. Voicing such imperatives is seen as beyond the scientists' pay grade and/or as a potential threat to their funding. So they leave them, by default, to political or religious bodies whose expertise is open to question. Meanwhile scientists get on with investigating, analyzing, and presenting data-based proof to their peers for whatever premise they are advancing: one that usually assumes or endorses our presumed genetic, rational, religious entitlement to appropriate and use all planetary resources to our own ends.

The disastrous effects that have followed from this lacuna in professional scientific leadership range from contaminated soil and water to mountaintop mining and deep sea oil exploration, increasing the risks to our own existence. So demonstrating how "rational" we really are! Yet scientific research has proved the Oneness of that existence beyond all doubt; most notably by revealing Earth from space to our initially astonished, awestruck gaze. Since then, what we make of that revelation or how it should affect our conduct appears largely to depend on individual human responses, since that is what is appealed to economically and politically. In the case of the former, we are told,

7. Ibid., 111–13.

for example, that our economic future depends in large part on increasing demands on and access to global resources.

So "Oneness" remains a scientific premise that, by its very order of magnitude, appears beyond any authoritative consensus as to how we are to respond to it. What is good and the right in the light of this premise remains an unspoken challenge that politicians and religious leaders, even more than scientists, are reluctant to express or to face, for fear of being seen as biased toward any collectively costly response.

This cultural reluctance is ultimately based on and upheld by the mental category of human uniqueness: upheld on the grounds either of our rational faculties or, religiously, on our possession of an immortal soul. So who can argue convincingly for a global response to the effects of climate change? Since the first Rio Conference on the Environment in 1992, the argument has essentially been preempted by economic forces that presuppose a lifestyle whose planetary costs cannot be supported but must still be shared by all. Government-sponsored science and economics effectively defaults on responding in an ecologically positive way to the reality of "One Earth" as the life resource base for all its living beings.

Meanwhile, the religious Christian *koinon*, in its many official forms, prays for world peace while investing large amounts of its pension funds in mining corporations, futures markets, and weapons manufacture. This would have come as no surprise to Leo Baeck. In his lifetime, the Christian churches in Germany not only supported the greatest human military machine in twentieth-century history: they also acquired particular infamy by supporting policies aimed at exterminating its Jewish subjects. In his first "Memorandum on the Jews" in September 1919, Hitler had already distinguished between an "antisemitism for purely emotional reasons," which would find expression in pogroms, and a "rational antisemitism" which must lead to "systematic legal struggle against and removal of the privileges of the Jew."

In his magisterial study *The Churches and the Third Reich*, Klaus Scholder notes that, during March 1933, internal and external legal changes took place at the end of which Protestantism publicly endorsed the Nationalist revolution and Catholicism offered a thinly disguised capitulation to it. In both churches at that time the decision was taken that no comment would be made on the terrorism of the new system and, in particular, on the persecution of the Jews now beginning in Germany.

> This decision did not go unchallenged, nor was it made in a day.
> Rather, it was the result of a development in which political and

church-political arguments gained the upper hand over simple Christian responsibility.[8]

The legal changes based on "rational antisemitism" were argued for on the basis of *human* difference, that is, on having one's heredity defined by the Jewish race in contrast to the smaller Central European races: out of which, according to Lutheran tradition, the German "Volk" was formed. The church's position was determined "not by political factors," but rather by "participation in the sacraments." While in retrospect, says Scholder, this may seem incomprehensible, inadequate and even scandalous, during the 1920s there had been a plethora of special laws for racial as well as ethnic minorities throughout the civilized world; without the political and church public feeling that this was a basic abrogation of the rule of law. It was no accident that Otto Dibelius rejected the intervention and criticism of the American churches in regard to the treatment of the Jews with the argument that the German churches were not intervening in the Negro question.[9]

What remained largely unexpressed within the official Christian churches, or even considered, was the striking similarity between the social position of Jesus in Palestine, the Jews in Germany, and that of the vast majority of American negroes.[10] Those German and American pastors who did express pastoral concern on these grounds saw that Christians had drawn great guilt upon themselves by keeping silent when they should have spoken out. Neither Protestant nor Roman Catholic Churches took part in political resistance to Hitler's policies in the strict sense, though there were numerous personal links with it. So those who resisted, like the Protestant pastor Dietrich Bonhoeffer and the Jesuit priest Alfred Delp, were outsiders in the two churches.[11]

This structural moral failure within the Christian *koinon* has already been discussed in relation to European colonization and has long been painfully evident to indigenous colonized peoples. Negro Christian scholar Howard Thurman describes being sent as an American delegate to a conference in 1935 at the University of Colombo, Ceylon, on the subject of "civil disabilities under states' rights in the United States." The Hindu principal invited him to coffee and asked:

> What are you doing over here? . . . More than three hundred years
> ago your forefathers were taken from the western coasts of Africa

8. Scholder, *The Churches and the Third Reich*, 254–55.

9. Ibid., 375.

10. Thurman, *Jesus and the Disinherited*, 34.

11. Scholder, *A Requiem for Hitler and Other New Perspectives on the German Church Struggle*, 118–19.

as slaves. The people who dealt in the slave traffic were Christians. One of your famous Christian hymn writers, Sir John Newton, made his money from the sale of slaves to the New World. He is the man who wrote "How Sweet the Name of Jesus Sounds" and "Amazing Grace." . . . The name of one of the famous British slave vessels was "Jesus." . . . I am a Hindu. I do not understand. Here you are in my country, standing deep within the Christian faith and tradition. . . . I think you are a traitor to all the darker peoples of the earth. I wonder what you, an intelligent man, can say in defence of your position.[12]

Their subsequent conversation, said Thurman, lasted five hours. He began with the simple historical fact that Jesus was a Jew and that it is impossible to understand him outside the sense of community that Israel held with God. How different, Thurman exclaimed, might have been the story of the last two thousand years if the link between Jesus and Israel had never been severed! The second important fact is that Jesus was a poor Jew. The economic predicament with which he was identified by birth placed him within the great mass of human beings on earth. The third fact is that he was a member of a minority group within the control of the dominant force of the Roman Empire.

All these, said Thurman, are important. They may tell us why Jesus was a particular kind of Jew but not why some other Jews were not Jesus. The urgent question for him was his attitude toward Rome. Attitudes varied from nonresistance and assimilation (Herod) to armed resistance (Zealots) to the prophetic (Jesus).

Jesus has a different alternative, expressed in his brief formula: "The kingdom of heaven is within us." . . . The basic fact is that Christianity as it was born in the mind of this Jewish teacher and thinker appears as a technique of survival for the oppressed. That it became, through the intervening years, a religion of the powerful and dominant, used sometimes as an instrument of oppression, must not tempt us into believing that it was thus in the mind of Jesus.[13]

This accords with the Jewish religious basis of Baeck's "One Thing"—and with the trajectory of his life. It also accords with the discussions in previous chapters about the role played by *koinonic* Christianity in appropriating, colonizing, monetizing, and devaluing the Earth. In the context of this chapter, it also accords with the history of the churches during the Holocaust. It brings into

12. Thurman, *Jesus and the Disinherited*, 15.
13. Ibid., 18–29.

sharper focus the contrasting and essential role played by exercising *koinonia,* by cultivating unity *between all living creatures* on the basis of God's indiscriminate love for them. Whatever our individual relationship with God, the sun, the rain, and planetary resources, these nourish our lives *together with* the lives of all creatures, regardless of species, race, creed, or power. That is the fundamental religious and scientific basis for our Earthly Oneness and therefore, for living peaceably.[14]

It is also at the heart of Baeck's "new principle," the "One Thing" demanded of us now more urgently (if implicitly) by science than by religion. On either basis, it means raising awareness of living in an already unified and inescapably interdependent earth community; and then rising to the challenges posed by that reality. Now more than ever, the challenge is a moral as well as a scientific one. Scientists don't do "moral imperatives." Yet they too cannot escape the fact that their findings on climate change demand "One Thing" from us: peaceful co-existence between our human selves and between us and all other species within our planetary home.

Within major Christian communities, preserving this basic earthly unity has not been seen, as it was by Jesus or by Baeck, as a categorical religious imperative that demands a collective as well as a personal response.[15] In both their cases, it was primarily a response to their experience of *disunity* in one of its most potent forms: that of being judged as outside the accepted human community on account of one's racial or religious heredity. In Jesus's case, it meant being a subject Jew within the Roman *koinon*: and not what he has become within the ecclesiastical *koinon*: a religious heavenly "object" revered by Christians as a guarantor of their eternal salvation, rather than the inspiration for living out of concern for the good of an all-inclusive earthly community. Unlike Paul he was not a Roman citizen, therefore like so many of the poor today he was not protected by the normal guarantees of citizenship. As was to be the case later for his fellow Jews in Germany and for displaced peoples worldwide. He did not have that quiet sense of security that comes from knowing that you "belong" within a unified society of property owners and the general sense of confidence that that inspires:

> If a Roman soldier pushed Jesus into a ditch, he could not appeal
> to Caesar; he would be just another Jew in the ditch—perpetually
> exposed to all the "arrows of outrageous fortune." . . . What stark
> insecurity! What a breeder of complete civil and moral nihilism
> and psychic anarchy! Unless one actually lives day by day without

14. Primavesi, *Cultivating Unity*, 80–97.
15. Baeck, *God and Man in Judaism*, 25.

a sense of security, he cannot understand what worlds separated
Jesus from Paul at this point.[16]

So, says Howard Thurman, he had to find some other basis upon which to
establish a sense of well-being. The goals of religion as he understood them
could never be worked out within the then-established imperial order. Deep
from within that order he projected a dream, the logic of which would give
needful security to all and through which no man would be a threat to another. For hatred is destructive to hater and hated alike. So "Love your enemy,"
that you may be children of your Father who sends rain and sunshine on Roman, Jew, and Christian alike.

Historically, this command to do what is good and right as far as possible to everyone regardless of race, religion, gender, sexual orientation, and, I
would add, species, has been more breached than observed throughout Christian history. The failure to discern the evil of racial, religious, gender, sexual,
and species discrimination throughout European Christian development and
colonization has scarred and continues to scar the unity of all earthly life.
Historically, the challenge has been met most consistently and successfully
by Buddhist nations, Gandhi-inspired political movements, and peace-based
Christian religious communities. Rejecting the militant theology of the *koinon* embodied in Roman imperial Christianity and its offshoots, the latter
try to embody in different ways Jesus's vision of a positive, life-enhancing
response to God's indiscriminate gifts that sustain the community of life in
all its diversity.

This religious logic now resounds back to us from the growing scientific
understanding of our belonging within a community dependent for life on its
planetary resource base. But it needs to be amplified religiously and culturally.
It has a strong contemporary echo in the life and work of the Jewish musician,
Daniel Barenboim. He has devoted himself to reconnecting the lives of Muslim and Jewish communities through the unifying power of music and, by doing so, has given us a musical paradigm of how to live harmoniously with and
through difference. To explain to ourselves the foundation of our existence,
he says, it is essential to understand the difference between force and power,
which he relates to the distinction between volume and intensity in music.

When a musician is told to play with greater intensity, his first reaction
is to play louder. In fact, the opposite is required: the lower the volume, the
greater the need for intensity; the greater the volume, the less the need for
intensity. The effect produced by the huge outpouring of sound in Beethoven
or Wagner is much greater when the sound is not forcefully controlled every

16. Thurman, *Jesus and the Disinherited*, 33–35.

step of the way, but rather allowed to grow organically, its natural, inherent power being the result of gradually accumulating strength. The build-up and release of tension are central to the expression of music.

> One must be able to hear the opposition, the notes that oppose the main idea. . . . In a perfectly harmonized ensemble in Mozart's operas, every single voice is simultaneously saying something completely different. . . . Music would be totally uninteresting without this sense of distinct elements. Even at a moment when everything comes together in a single chord, one must be able to hear all the different voices.[17]

This sensory perception of unified difference is not confined to our ears. It is before our eyes whenever we look at a landscape; discerned by our taste when we eat; by our touch when we reach out to another body; by our nose when we walk through a garden. It belongs with and reacts to our earthiness. It happens because, as the title of Barenboim's book states: everything is connected. We need to demonstrate and experience this truth in as many ways as possible.

17. Barenboim, *Everything Is Connected*, 131–32.

12

Living Earth

Seen in all its shining beauty against the deep darkness of space, the Earth looks very much alive. This impression of life is real. Only a planet with abundant life, and able to retain its water and regulate its unique atmosphere and climate, could appear so different from its sister planets, Mars and Venus, both of which are dead.[1]

In the fall of 2012, communities in the Caribbean and along the eastern shores of the United States had to deal with the effects of Hurricane Sandy that drove millions of people from their homes. Attention was largely focused on its effects along "the ancient world of the shore," as Rachel Carson called the eastern Atlantic Coast of North America. There, she said, for as long as there has been earth and sea, the land and water have met and kept alive "the sense of continuing creation and the relentless drive of life." That relentlessness was very much to the fore in Sandy. In calmer times Carson found deeper meanings on that shoreland which she described as the "intricate fabric of life by which one creature is linked with another, and each with its surroundings."[2]

This belief in our being linked with one another and with our environment differs from the standard view. We usually see ourselves in terms of difference from others on grounds of race, religion and gender, focusing on our

1. Lovelock, *Gaia: The Practical Science of Planetary Medicine*, 36.
2. Carson, *The Edge of the Sea*, 11.

personal identity within the human community and seeing it in human terms alone. We also differentiate between ourselves and creatures inhabiting the seas because we belong naturally to the land. In short, we view ourselves in terms of difference from each other and from the natural environment, seeing it as subject to weather changes but, on the whole, relating to it as a backdrop to our lives rather than an active agent in continuously creating and driving them forward.

Like Carson, that is, from a scientific viewpoint, James Lovelock sensed and investigated the linkages between us and these environmental life forces at a global as well as a personal level. Both expressed their sense of connectedness with the unique atmosphere and climate of Earth; in her case with the great tides ebbing and flowing along the shore. She noted that their progress was visibly marked by stripes of color running parallel to the sea's edge composed of living things. These reflected the stages of the tide: the length of time that a particular level of shore remains uncovered and so determines, in large measure, what life forms it can support. With only minor variations, she said, this pattern exists in all parts of the world:

> Contemplating the teeming life of the shore, we have an uneasy
> sense of the communication of some universal truth that lies just
> beyond our grasp. The meaning haunts and ever eludes us, and in
> its very pursuit we approach the ultimate mystery of Life itself.[3]

This universal truth, that Earth's Life connects us not only with the life of planet Earth but also with each other and with all living creatures, is the ultimate mystery of our Gaian oneness whose reality lies beyond words. Different perceptions of its truth at different times and places have evoked a variety of human responses ranging from the worship of the Greek Earth Goddess Gaia to her disdain and death within the Roman *koinon*. That disdain has found lethal religious expression throughout human history, notably in Christian colonizations where indigenous peoples' worshipful relationship with the land was utterly disdained by those who appropriated it as their property, relating to it and to its life forms solely as a source of monetary gain.

Now religious differences based on rival truth claims by Christians and Muslims are a major factor in the destruction of those same earthly resources that support the lives of their communities.

> Believing that one's religion is the ultimate truth and infinitely
> superior to others can easily lead to intolerance, prejudice, and
> exclusivity. When this kind of belief is combined with racial and

3. Ibid., 31–34, 216.

ethnic bigotry, perceived discrimination and injustice, and the
hope for political revenge, violence and even holy war may occur.[4]

And with it, devastation of both the lives and life resources of those who hold
different religious views. Yet Leo Baeck's vision of the One and Jesus's vision
of the kingdom of God, based on the oneness of all creatures on Earth, offer a
very different, peaceful response to others' religious claims:

> If your leaders tell you
> "Look! This presence [God's kingdom] is in the skies!"
> Remember,
> The birds who fly the skies have known this all along.
> If they say,
> "It is in the seas!"
> Remember,
> Dolphins and fish have always known it.
> It is not apart from you.
> It wells up within each and surrounds all. (Gospel of Thomas 3)[5]

Perceiving the truth of our connectedness evoked a musical response from
Daniel Barenboim and a biologist's response from Rachel Carson. In 1979,
the scientific technologies developed for space travel allowed James Lovelock
to endorse these ancient and modern observations of and reactions to the
"mystery of life":

> The idea of Mother Earth or, as the Greeks called her, Gaia, has
> been widely held throughout history and has been the basis of
> a belief that coexists with the great religions. Ancient belief and
> modern wisdom have fused emotionally in the awe with which
> astronauts with their own eyes and we with television have seen
> the Earth revealed in all its shining beauty against the deep dark-
> ness of space.[6]

True to the scientific spirit of his age, Lovelock noted that this feeling, however
strong, did not prove that Mother Earth lives. So he explored the concept of
the Earth as a kind of living superorganism: as being able to regulate its climate and composition so as always to be comfortable for life in all its forms.
He did this, he noted, in a most respectable scientific environment: the Jet
Propulsion Laboratory in California, where contemporary space exploration
posed questions about the composition of the air we share with all creatures

4. Kwok, *Globalization, Gender and Peacebuilding*, 69.

5. (Mark Primavesi's rendering.)

6. Lovelock, *Gaia: A New Look at Life on Earth*, xiv.

when we breathe. He looked for answers by studying Earth's atmosphere from the top down, from space. This was in line with NASA plans to look for life on Mars: based on the assumption that the evidence for that would be much the same as for life on Earth.[7]

So the primary question became: Why is there life on Earth? Seeking an answer led Lovelock to formulate Gaia theory, which assumes that everything alive on Earth is ultimately and intricately connected to Earth's own life-force:

> Gaia is the Earth seen as a single physiological system, an entity that is alive at least to the extent that, like other living organisms, its chemistry and temperature are self-regulated at a state favourable for life.[8]

Now we accept, theoretically at least, that Hurricane Sandy was part of that single physiological system: no less alive for our being able to predict its speed and direction, to slot it into a particular category of force and to measure its impact on an agreed scale. Its damaging power also reminded us that while we may be able to analyze its force scientifically, it belongs to a global system that remains beyond our control. At that level, it is unconstrained by any human, religious, or national boundary but is part of the life-generating, interactive self-organizing matter that constitutes all Earthly lifeforms; from the seed buried in the ground to subvisible microorganisms in the ocean depths to the blood in our veins.

As such, it is indeed worthy of our awe. Lovelock's close friend and collaborator, Lynn Margulis, describes life's planetary composition:

> Twenty kilometers thick, its top is the atmosphere and its bottom is continental rock and ocean depths. Life's body is like a tree trunk. Only its outermost tissues grow. . . . Life, as far as is known, is limited to the surface of this third planet from the sun. Moreover, this living matter utterly depends on the sun, a medium-sized star in the outback of the Milky Way Galaxy.[9]

This is an up-to-date description of Teilhard de Chardin's "mighty matter" in the epigraph to the preface. I do like Margulis relegating our Sun to the "outback" of the Milky Way Galaxy! So much for our pretensions about "our" planet, Earth, being at the center of the Universe. Yet it is also true that, as far as our knowledge goes, that is, as far as it has been extended by science and space exploration, solar-dependent human-like life exists only on Earth. And

7. Ibid., xiv–xv.

8. Lovelock, *Gaia: the Practical Science of Planetary Medicine*, 11.

9. Margulis and Sagan, *What Is Life?*, 14.

because Earth is alive, every life form, including ourselves, belongs to Life's body within the biosphere that is the product of billions of years of interactions between chemically-related systems and their environments. Through those interactions all life forms, including ours, have coevolved into the living beings that exist today. This life-bearing planet keeps us and all other earthly bodies alive through a single coevolutionary process between all of us and our environments.

In Gaia theory, this process is called "tight coupling": the close relationship between the coevolution of living organisms and their physical and chemical environments. Throughout this whole process, changes occur in both bodily organisms and environments that are an expression of their own structural dynamics and of their selective interactions with others. In poetic terms, these drive a flower upwards from its roots into the sun. In climate sciences, they drive a hurricane through the sea and onto the land. In both cases, interactive components coevolve within a process that allows us to describe them separately.[10]

In the latter case, extreme climatic effects are in a continuity of relationships resulting from the long-term impact on our planetary resource base of our appropriation, colonization, industrialization, monetization, marketization, and militarization of Earth's resources. All of which may be seen as a tacit rejection of the boundaries of that resource base: on the grounds that human beings are special or closer to God or that our intellect has "lifted us" above the natural world into a more congenial, human-created environment. At the same time, we are becoming more and more aware that our absolute need for air, water, soil, energy, and biodiversity belies these assumptions:

> These days, many people believe that science and technology provide us with the understanding and tools to manage nature and to find solutions to problems that science and technology have helped to create. . . . Some people believe that a clean environment is only affordable when the economy is strong, but in fact, it's the other way round; the biosphere is what gives us life and a living.[11]

So, highlighted by major events like Hurricane Sandy, there is a growing awareness of *Earth's* uniqueness in respect to its richness and diversity of life forms, including our own. Such an awareness compels us to make a necessary re-evaluation of our own earthiness that, rather than disdaining it, sees it instead as the source of whatever life and beauty there is for us. True, religious attribution of its creation to God goes beyond any scientific hypothesis. But

10. Primavesi, *Sacred Gaia*, 3–5.
11. Suzuki and McConnell, *The Sacred Balance*, 211–12.

then so does the reality of Earth itself. And, as Kwok points out, the concept of divine multiplicity is characterized by fluidity because it is ever-changing, without closures and endings. Learning to become fluent in our speaking of God implies a willingness to enter into a flow of language without closures and endings.[12]

Such a religious vision of Earth's all-embracing presence not only amplifies but gives voice to our appreciation of how, ultimately, the *origin* of life within our universe remains a mystery to scientists also. In 1944, Howard Thurman, a black pastor, admirably conveyed this sense of appreciation:

> The earth beneath my feet is the great womb out of which the life upon which my body depends comes in utter abundance. There is at work in the soil a mystery by which the death of one seed is reborn a thousandfold in newness of life. . . . [I]t is order, and more than order—there is a brooding tenderness out of which it all comes. In the contemplation of the earth, I know that I am surrounded by the love of God.[13]

Thurman resolutely took his stand on the Earth and in the here and now. And on that basis, refused to downgrade earthly bodies or any form of earthly life (whether our own or that of other-than-human creatures) in favor of a "future" unearthly, disembodied existence located beyond the biosphere. It is worth remembering that the mental category "soul," whether used philosophically or religiously, has always implied, indeed required its "oneness" with a human body. Similarly the mental category "heaven" makes no sense unless seen and experienced from Earth within a planetary universe beyond our mental or physical grasp. And while within the Christian *koinon* a male God is Ruler of a hierarchical, vertical paradigmatic order of being with Earth at its base, even here, that order remains *One*.

It is also true, however, that in secular governmental hierarchies (on which the vertical religious category is modeled) it is one's closeness to or distance from the imperial apex that decides one's order of importance. This ranking has determined not only our relationship with each other but also with Earth. So, as evidenced in the account of the death of Socrates, Western cultural perceptions of human identity have upheld the supremacy of key male figures whilst life-bearing females are associated with the mute ground inhabited by the living natural world. Global governmental meetings and those of major religious groups embody this paradigm as they customarily give precedence to male human governance, implicitly endorsing the subordination

12. Kwok, *Globalization, Gender and Peacebuilding*, 73.
13. Thurman, *Meditations of the Heart*, 210–11.

of women and other-than-human species and automatically downgrading Earth's body to utilitarian status.

This hierarchical disdain for the most fundamental, life-giving aspects of our earthiness has taken many forms, philosophical, political and religious, that have, over time, fostered and supported basic cultural tenets about human lives (or rather, some of them) in distinction from those of all other "earthy" bodies. Within mainstream Christianity, these tenets have included *opposing* categories of body-soul, body-mind, earth-spirit, male-female in which primacy is given to soul, mind, spirit, and male. Religiously and culturally this harks back to such adaptations of philosophy as the early Christian poet Valentinus and his reflections on the opening verses of John's Gospel:

> All things I see suspended through spirit;
> All things borne along through spirit;
> Flesh depending on soul,
> Soul bound to air
> Air depending on ether.[14]

Although later branded a heretic, Valentinus showed how, though rarely directly invoked, Greek philosophical traditions affected early Christian religious culture, especially in reading the Bible solely as a history of humanity and in assuming that we are composites of inferior earthy bodies and superior minds, souls, or spirits. So while this attitude is culturally redundant in the light of what we now know and accept scientifically about our evolution as an earthly species, it remains strong enough to shape present Christian teaching and western cultural attitudes to our earthiness and bodiliness. And although Valentinus's reading of John's Gospel raised Irenaeus's ire, its philosophical roots continue to find support in a correlation between the image of God and "man" that remains largely unquestioned, despite the work of Hebrew scholars such as Mary Phil Korsak and Carol Meyers:

> We will make a groundling (adam)
> In our image, after our likeness.[15] (Genesis 1:26)

To translate *adam* as "man," says Carol Meyers, is to imply a priority for male existence and also to ignore a magnificent Hebrew wordplay. The word for the stuff from which the first human being is formed is *adamah*, usually translated as "ground" or "earth." The words for "human" and for "ground" are thus connected phonetically and perhaps also etymologically. Texts such as Genesis 2:7, in their traditional English translations, do not preserve or communicate

---

14. Pagels, *Adam, Eve and the Serpent*, 115–16.

15. Translated by Korsak, *At the Start: Genesis Made New*, 4–5.

either the generic use of "man" or the integral connection of humanity with its earthly matrix: with that layer of "mighty matter" that contains and nourishes the unity of earthly life.

In order to capture the flavor and meaning of the original text, such verses ought to be rendered something like:

> Then God Yahweh formed an earthling of clods from the earth
> and breathed into its nostril the breath of life; and the earthling
> became a living being.

Or:

> Then God Yahweh formed a human from clods of the humus and
> breathed into its nostrils the breath of life, and the human became
> a living being.

After all, Meyers says, the English "human" is not the combination of *hu* and *man* but rather is derived from a theoretical Indo-European root (*ghum*) meaning "earth" or "ground"; from which comes the Latin *humus* and Old English *guma* (man).[16] However, these human genetic markers (soil, ground, life, flesh, breath, soul) were read and have been used and interpreted by both Christians and non-Christians as that which distinguishes humans from all other living species. Religiously and culturally, this has meant that even though this attitude is redundant in the light of what we now know and accept scientifically about our earthly evolution, primacy has been given to "cultivating" the soul or mind at the expense of the body in all its forms.

While we may assume that such biblical translations and their presuppositions would most likely have been unknown to the Lambeth workman who inscribed the earthenware hand-warmer in 1672, they resonated then and continue to resonate now with much Christian belief. Also, by his lifetime they had had a philosophical, cultural and indeed practical influence on his contemporary, the philosopher John Locke, which not only affected his own attitudes to Earth but have had enduring effects on the global landscape to this day. Previous chapters have explored how Locke made and used distinctions between soul and body, mind and earth, in order to conclude: *As the mind owns the body, so a person owns property.* This became a central tenet of a liberalism whose effects on the bodies of all species, human and other-than-human, and on the "mighty matter" of Earth's body, are now all too visible.

For Locke, "Earth" meant "property," human property, and to a large extent, it still does. This has meant that other-than-human creatures are routinely considered to be without minds or souls; to belong to Earth's resources

16. Meyers, *Discovering Eve*, 81–82.

and so to exist solely as a source of monetary profit and as a human social and bodily supply base. The science of his day gave Locke a terminology that updated his philosophical and religious views of the "bodiliness" of the land. It is, he said, a form of physical property: an aggregate of atoms comprising a material substance that follows the laws of physics and exists in space and time. Minds, however, that is, human minds, are immaterial, independent and self-sufficient mental substances that exist outside of space and time.[17]

Reading this now may make us smile. But in fact, whether in the U.S. Founders' Constitution or in university curricula, Locke's mind and its activities *do* still live on long after his time. Otherwise, their effects would not have been examined here in such depth nor would he have been so extensively quoted. But we now know that his mind was neither independent of his space and time nor was it self-sufficient. How much of its enduring power has been due to the appeal of this self-image and its general acceptance by others? How many other theories with a contrary view of ourselves have perished? This phase-change in personal attitudes to Earth as a living body was discussed in chapter 4. Locke's perceptions continue to hold power wherever an inferred distinction between earthly mortality and immortality of the mind or soul supports policies or attitudes that downgrade our own "earthiness" in favor of the accumulation and inheritance of property and future monetary "gain." Hierarchical Christian institutions support these distinctions doctrinally and symbolically by stressing the importance for our "souls" of being "heirs" to some deferred "treasure in heaven."

This double cultural effect encourages us to ignore the fact that our earthiness is literally the gift of life to us. No other way of being alive exists. The life forces within and outside the seed that drive its growth into a living organism is Earth's unique gift to it and to all within the biosphere—including ourselves. In spite of the best endeavors of scientists using the latest and most sophisticated technology, life is still in Earth's gift alone. And continues to be so even though the ancient identification of Earth as Gaia, a nurturing mother, gradually vanished as a dominant image during a Scientific Revolution that systematized and rationalized the life processes of all organic life, including our own.

Nevertheless, as biologist and artist Glynn Gorick has found, the differences between human systems of economic accounting and natural flows within the planetary biosphere of energy and materials are such that the process of "giving" in its true sense remains outside a human economic view. Life or energy is "given" without any design for feedback:

17. Chappell, ed., *The Cambridge Companion to Locke*, 27–29, 56.

> [I]t is not logical, not scientific or physics; maybe it is in the realm
> of metaphysics. I have a feeling that this is a quality of very high
> power that is not measurable and plays a huge role in the evolution
> and stability/security of communities. [18]

From this perspective, *giving* life to all organisms, species and plants is Earth's defining characteristic. And as Earth is definitely *not* our property, neither is life. We do not own earth's life-giving resources nor can we harness its "force" other than in a most transitory and minimal sense. Within a relatively short time in human history, we have learnt that "what we now are" results from incremental changes in what we have been and in the environments that have nourished our lives over time. As Darwin saw, "whilst this planet has gone cycling on according to the fixed law of gravity," genetic and geographical differences have created "endless forms most beautiful and most wonderful." Now "these elaborately constructed forms, so different from each other and so dependent on each other in so complex a manner" can be and are being mapped with increasing accuracy.[19]

But we do not own them. They are not our property; just as the Earth we share with them is not our property. It is our life. A positive affirmation of this truth was presented twenty years ago to the first 1992 UNCED meeting in Rio in the original NGO Earth Charter and in the foundation document of the Suzuki Foundation. These may be found in the Appendices.

18. Primavesi, *Gaia's Gift*, 112.
19. Darwin, *The Origin of Species*, 459.

Afterword

The Gift of Gaian Identity

We humans have traditionally and routinely described our ancestry and identity within the narrow terms of human communities and citizenship; of familial, national, political, or religious genealogies. James Lovelock's Gaia theory expands the breadth of our self-understanding; situating us where our ancestry and present identity are actually grounded: within the evolutionary lineages and environments of the whole Earth community. He named this Earth community "Gaia," describing it as a superorganism in which all life is tightly coupled with air, ocean, and surface rocks.

In this whole that is more than the sum of its parts there is no question of human life being external to or independent of that whole. To imagine and to act out our human identity as if it were outside of or in control of Gaia's self-regulatory functioning, its common environmental and climatic variables or ecosystem constraints, is now seen for what it is: so serious a misunderstanding of how we are constituted as to put our survival, never mind our thriving, in gravest danger.

In fact, a Gaian human identity is a gift given us at birth; one given from and within the entire history of life's emergence on this planet. It went largely unnoticed throughout much of our lives. But Gaia theory enlarged our vision with a truth about ourselves that compelled a radical shift in our self-understanding. It extended our historic perspective on the past, present, and future beyond that of family, race, country, church, or nation.

With this wider vision came a growing awareness that our past and present are inextricably linked: not just to the past and future of one particular evolutionary lineage but to that of all life on Earth. All living beings now on Earth are literally related. We may be closest to African apes. But we are also related, albeit more distantly, to mice and fish and beetles, to worms and mushrooms and oak trees . . . and so on to the tiniest bacterium.

And each of these is not only related to but tightly coupled with the environments of other life forms; interrelated to them and co-arising with them. Each life depends on the work and gifts of other lives; of those who once lived and those alive today. Each is bound ineluctably to all others past and present in a continuing cycle of birth, life, and death that sustains each within all. Our relatedness to all forms of life is at the heart of our Gaian identity.

Gaia theory has shown us how to trace that identity back, however sketchily, through Earth's history, marveling at the uniqueness of our own lives while sensing the strange relatedness of others. Knowing that we remain related to them through the air we breathe, the solar energy we share, the components of soil, atmosphere, and water that nourish us in life and to which we all contribute both in life and in death.

This relatedness in all its forms is the present source and sustenance of our physical being and of all other living entities. It is, therefore, the source of our id-entity: of the sameness (*idem*) of being (*ens*) that creates and sustains our Gaian being. Together we continually contribute, for good or ill, to that identity. Through it we share in the mutual benefits of a common life that we in turn continually create—or destroy.

Our home is within Earth's biosphere: that Gaian space structured by concentric spheres surrounding the planet. Solar energy heats the atmosphere and oceans, driving the global circulation of these two planetary systems. Like skin and fur, the atmosphere keeps Earth's surface warm. It also shields the delicate living cells of the surface against exposure to solar radiation. Earth's magnetic field prevents it from being blown away by solar winds.

This Gaian atmosphere evolved to be just thick enough for us to breathe but not so opaque as to absorb entirely the light from other bodies in the universe. Therefore we can breathe and we can see the stars. This fragile balance between the indispensable and the sublime gives us an experience of transcendence on which to build our concepts and theories of what transcends us.

While Gaia theory offers us a scientific understanding of the structure and composition of the planetary environment and atmosphere that both transcends us and makes Earth habitable for us, it also allows us to glimpse the reality of the whole community of life within which we belong.

It enables us to see that community as embodying a sacredness that attaches to the whole of existence; and to see the sacred as the internal transcendence of all living beings. This is embodied in the tight coupling, the delicate balance within our Gaian identity between what is indispensable for our continuance as individuals and what we intuit as the sacredness of the whole of existence.

Appendix 1

The Original NGO Earth Charter

Prepared by the non-governmental organizations gathered together in Rio de Janeiro for the United Nations Conference on Environment and Development, June 3–14, 1992.

Preamble

We are the Earth, the people, plants and animals, rains and oceans, breath of the forest and flow of the sea.

We honor Earth as the home of all living things.

We cherish Earth's beauty and diversity of life.

We welcome Earth's ability to renew as being the basis of all life.

We recognize the special place of Earth's Indigenous Peoples, their territories, their customs and their unique relationship to Earth.

We are appalled at the human suffering, poverty and damage to Earth caused by inequality of power.

We accept a shared responsibility to protect and restore Earth and to allow wise and equitable use of resources so as to achieve an ecological balance and new social, economic and spiritual values.

In all our diversity we are one. Our common home is increasingly threatened. We thus commit ourselves to the following principles, noting at all times the particular needs of women, indigenous peoples, the South, the disabled and all those who are disadvantaged:

Principles

1. We agree to respect, encourage, protect and restore Earth's ecosystems to ensure biological and cultural diversity.

2. We recognize our diversity and our common partnership. We respect all cultures and affirm the rights of all people to basic environmental needs.

3. Poverty affects us all. We agree to alter unsustainable patterns of production and consumption to ensure the eradication of poverty and to end the abuse of Earth. This must include a recognition of the role of debt and financial flows from the South to the North and opulence and corruption as primary causes. We shall emphasize and improve the endogenous capacity for technology creation and development. Attempts to eradicate poverty should not be a mandate to abuse the environment and attempts to protect or restore the environment should not ignore basic human needs.

4. We recognize that national barriers do not generally conform to Earth's ecological realities. National sovereignty does not mean sanctuary from our collective responsibility to protect and restore Earth's ecosystems. Trade practices and transnational corporations must not cause environmental degradation and should be controlled in order to achieve social justice, equitable trade solidarity with ecological principles.

5. We reject the buildup and use of military force and the use of economic pressure as means of resolving conflict. We commit ourselves to pursue genuine peace, which is not merely the absence of war but includes the eradication of poverty, the promotion of social justice and economic, spiritual, cultural, and ecological well-being.

6. We agree to ensure that decision-making processes and their criteria are clearly defined, transparent, explicit, accessible and equitable. Those whose decisions or activities may affect the environment must first prove the absence of harm. Those likely to be affected, particularly populations in the South and those in subjugation within existing States, should have free access to information and effectively participate in the decision-making processes.

7. States, institutions, corporations, and peoples are unequal in their contribution to environmental harm, experience of ecological degradation and ability to respond to environmental destruction. While all are responsible for improving environmental quality, those who have expropriated or consumed the majority of Earth's resources or who continue

to do so must cease such expropriation or reduce such consumption and must bear the costs of ecological restoration and protection by providing the majority of financial and technological resources.

8. Women constitute over half of Earth's human population. They are a powerful source for change. They contribute more than half the effort to human welfare. Men and women agree that women's status in decision-making and social processes must equitably reflect their contribution. We must shift from a society dominated by men to one which more accurately reflects the valued contributions of men and women to human and ecological welfare.

We have come to realize that the threats to the biosphere which sustains all live on Earth have increased in rate, magnitude and scale to such extent that inaction would be negligent.

Earth Charter Action Plan

1. We shall adopt the spirit and principles of the Earth Charter at the individual level and through concrete actions within our Non-Governmental Organizations.

2. We will use existing mechanisms and/or create an international network of the signatories here to disseminate the Earth Charter as principles for action at the local, national, and global level.

3. The Earth Charter shall be translated into all the languages of Earth.

4. We shall commit ourselves to preparation of "OBJECTIVE 1995" by which the United Nations will celebrate its 50th anniversary, at which time we want them to adopt this Earth Charter.

5. Non-Governmental Organizations worldwide shall initiate a combined campaign "WE ARE EARTH" through to 1995 and the adoption of this Earth Charter by the United Nations.

6. Every individual, organization, corporation, and state shall dedicate a percentage of their operating budget and their profit as an "Earth Percentage" dedicated to the restoration, protection, and management of Earth's ecosystems and promotion of equitable development.

7. We call for a second Global Forum to be held in 1999 to evaluate and reaffirm our commitment to the relationships made, the accomplishments achieved and the goals sought at this "1992 Global Forum."

This text of this first Earth Charter and how it was later "sanitized" may be found online: http://www.discerningtoday.org/members/Analyses/earth%20 charter.htm.

Appendix 2

David Suzuki Foundation Declaration of Interdependence

We, Anne and Mark Primavesi, have signed up to this Declaration of Inter-dependence, written in 1992 by David Suzuki, Tara Cullis, Raffi Cavoukian, Wade Davis, and others as the founding document of the David Suzuki Foundation.

The text of this document and the opportunity to sign up to it may be found on line at: http://www.davidsuzuki.org/about/declaration/

You may may also hear David Suzuki and Tara Cullis reading the decla-ration at: http://youtu.be/FeOU5vydSBY.

This We Know

We are the earth, through the plants and animals that nourish us.
We are the rains and the oceans that flow through our veins.
We are the breath of the forests of the land, and the plants of the sea.
We are human animals, related to all other life as descendants of the first-born cell.
We share with these kin a common history, written in our genes.
We share a common present, filled with uncertainty.
And we share a common future, as yet untold.
We humans are but one of thirty million species
weaving the thin layer of life enveloping the world.
The stability of communities of living things depends upon this diversity.
Linked in that web, we are interconnected—
using, cleansing, sharing and replenishing the fundamental elements of life.

Our home, planet Earth, is finite; all life shares its resources and the energy
from the sun, and therefore has limits to growth.
For the first time, we have touched those limits.
When we compromise the air, the water, the soil and the variety of life,
we steal from the endless future to serve the fleeting present.

This We Believe

Humans have become so numerous and our tools so powerful
that we have driven fellow creatures to extinction, dammed the great rivers,
torn down ancient forests, poisoned the earth, rain and wind, and ripped
holes in the sky.
Our science has brought pain as well as joy; our comfort is paid for by the
suffering of millions.
We are learning from our mistakes, we are mourning our vanished kin,
and we now build a new politics of hope.
We respect and uphold the absolute need for clean air, water and soil.
We see that economic activities that benefit the few while shrinking the
inheritance of many are wrong.
And since environmental degradation erodes biological capital forever,
full ecological and social cost must enter all equations of development.
We are one brief generation in the long march of time; the future is not ours
to erase.
So where knowledge is limited, we will remember all those who will walk
after us,
and err on the side of caution.

This We Resolve

All this that we know and believe must now become the foundation of the
way we live.
At this turning point in our relationship with Earth,
we work for an evolution: from dominance to partnership;
from fragmentation to connection; from insecurity,
to interdependence.

Bibliography

Auerbach, Eric. *Mimesis: The Representation of Reality in Western Literature.* Princeton: Princeton University Press, 2003.

Baeck, Leo. *God and Man in Judaism.* London: Valentine, Mitchell and Co., 1958.

Bakan, Joel. *The Corporation:* London: Constable, 2004.

Balasuriya, Tissa. *Planetary Theology.* London: SCM, 1984.

Balmford, Andrew. *Wild Hope: On the Front Lines of Conservation Success.* Chicago: University of Chicago Press, 2012.

Barenboim, Daniel. *Everything Is Connected: The Power of Music.* London: Weidenfeld and Nicholson, 2008.

Bateson, Gregory. *Steps to an Ecology of Mind.* New York: Ballantine, 1972.

Bramah, Ernest. *Kai Kung's Golden Hours.* Middlesex: Penguin, 1938.

Brockman, John. *The Third Culture.* New York: Touchstone, 1995.

Brown, Peter. *Through the Eye of a Needle: Wealth, the Fall of Rome, and the Making of Christianity in the West, 350–550 AD.* Princeton: Princeton University Press, 2012.

Browne, Janet. *The Secular Ark: Studies in the History of Biogeography.* New Haven: Yale University Press, 1983.

Bunyan, John. "*Pilgrim's Progress,* Part 1, the Seventh Stage." No pages. Online: http://www.whatsaiththescripture.com/Stories/Bunyan.Pilgrims.Progress7.html.

Caffentzis, Constantine George. *Clipped Coins, Abused Words and Civil Government.* New York: Autonomedia, 1989.

Carson, Rachel. *The Edge of the Sea.* New York: New American Library, 1955.

Cavarero, Adriana. *In Spite of Plato: A Feminist Rewriting of Ancient Philosophy.* Oxford: Polity, 1995.

Chappell, Vere, ed. *The Cambridge Companion to Locke.* Cambridge: Cambridge University Press, 1994.

Clarke, George. *John Bellars: His Life, Times and Writings.* London: Routledge and Kegan Paul, 1987.

Cooper, John M., ed. *Plato: Complete Works.* Indianapolis: Hackett, 1997.

Crossan, Dominic. *Jesus: A Revolutionary Biography.* San Francisco: Harper, 1994.

Darwin, Charles. *The Origin of Species by Means of Natural Selection.* Edited by W. J. Burrow. London: Penguin, 1859. Reprint, 1985.

de Chardin, Pierre Teilhard. *Hymn of the Universe.* Translated by Gerald Vann. London: Collins, 1965.

Descartes, Rene. *A Discourse on Method.* Translated by John Veitch. Edited by Ernest Rhys. First ed. Vol. 570. Everyman's Library. London:Dent, 1912.

Douglas-Klotz, Neil. *The Hidden Gospel: Decoding the Spiritual Message of the Aramaic Jesus.* Wheaton, IL: Quest, 1999.

Duchrow, Ulrich, and Franz J. Hinkelammert. *Property for People, Not for Profit.* London: Zed, 2004.

Ellis, William N. *A Gaian Paradigm.* N.P.: Xlibris, 2011.

Graeber, David. *Debt: The First 5,000 Years.* New York: Melville, 2011.

Hallman, David G., ed. *Ecotheology: Voices from South and North.* Maryknoll, NY: Orbis, 1994.

Hardy, Thomas. "Let Me Enjoy." No pages. Online: http://www.theotherpages.org/poems/hardy04.html.

Havelock, Eric A. *The Muse Learns to Write: Reflections on Orality and Literacy from Antiquity to the Present.* New Haven: Yale University Press, 1986.

———. *Preface to Plato.* Belknap Press ed. Cambridge, MA: Harvard University Press, 1963.

Hedges, Chris. *Days of Destruction, Days of Revolt.* New York: Nation, 2012.

Hopkins, Gerard Manley. *Poems.* Second ed. London: Oxford University Press, 1930.

Jennings, Theodore W. Jr. "John Wesley." In *Empire and the Christian Tradition: New Readings of Classical Theologians,* edited by Kwok Pui-lan, Don H. Compier, and Joerg Rieger, 256–69. Minneapolis: Fortress, 2007.

Kahl, Brigitte. *Galatians Re-Imagined: Reading with the Eyes of the Vanquished.* Minneapolis: Fortress, 2010.

Korsak, Mary Phil. *At the Start: Genesis Made New.* New York: Doubleday, 1993.

Krauss, Lawrence, M. "A Universe without Purpose." No pages. Online: http://old.richarddawkins.net/articles/645484-a-universe-without-purpose.

Kurland, P. B., and R. Lerner. "The Founders' Constitution." No pages. Online: http://press-pubs.uchicago.edu/founders/documents/introduction.html.

Kwok, Pui-lan. *Globalization, Gender and Peacebuilding: The Future of Interfaith Dialogue.* New York: Paulist, 2012.

La Chapelle, Dolores. *Sacred Land, Sacred Sex, Rapture of the Deep.* Silverton, CO: Finn Hill Arts, 1988.

Lambin, Eric. *An Ecology of Happiness.* Chicago: University of Chicago Press, 2012.

Laslett, Peter. *Locke: Two Treatises of Government.* Cambridge: Cambridge University Press, 1988.

Locke, John. *An Essay Concerning Human Understanding.* Glasgow: Collins, 1964.

Logan, William Bryant. *Dirt: The Ecstatic Skin of the Earth.* New York: Norton, 1995.

Lovelock, James. *Gaia: A New Look at Life on Earth.* Oxford: Oxford University Press, 1979.

———. *Gaia: The Practical Science of Planetary Medicine.* London: Gaia,, 1991.

Lozovsky, Natalia. *The Earth Is Our Book: Geographical Knowledge in the Latin West ca. 400–1000.* Ann Arbor: University of Michigan Press, 2000.

Luttwak, Edward. "The *Iliad* by Homer, Translated by Stephen Mitchell." Review of the *Iliad* by Homer, translated by Stephen Mitchell. *London Review of Books,* February 23, 2012, 3–8.

MacCulloch, Diarmaid. "Mumpsimus, Sumpsimus." Review of *Book of Common Prayer:* The Texts of 1549, 1559, 1662. Edited by Brian Cummings. *London Review of Books,* May 24, 2012, 13–15.

Margulis, Lynn, and Dorion Sagan. *What Is Life?* London: Weidenfeld & Nicholson, 1995.

Martinez-Vazquez, Hjamil A. "Bartolomé De Las Casas." In *Empire and the Christian Tradition: New Readings of Classical Theologians*, edited by Kwok Pui-lan, Don H. Compier, and Joerg Rieger, 201–14. Minneapolis: Fortress, 2007.

Meyers, Carol. *Discovering Eve: Ancient Israelite Women in Context.* Oxford: Oxford University Press, 1988.

Midgley, Mary. "On Being an Anthrozoon." No pages. Online: YouTube lecture: http://youtu.be/_pm3oaal38s; PDF file: http://www.isaz.net/conferences/Midgley%20plenary%20text.pdf.

———. *The Solitary Self.* Durham: Acumen, 2010.

Milton, John. "*Paradise Lost*, Book 1." No pages. Online: http://www.netpoets.com/classic/poems/045009.htm.

Monbiot, George. "Putting a Price on the Rivers and Rain Diminishes Us All." No pages. Online: http://www.guardian.co.uk/commentisfree/2012/aug/06/price-rivers-rain-greatest-privatisation.

Nelson, Stephanie A. *God and the Land: The Metaphysics of Farming in Hesiod and Vergil.* Oxford: Oxford University Press, 1998.

Norcross, Beth. "Eye on the Sparrow." No pages. Online: http://sojo.net/magazine/2012/08/eye-sparrow.

Pagels, Elaine. *Adam, Eve and the Serpent.* London: Penguin, 1990.

Plato. *Plato: Timaeus and Critias.* Translated by H. D. P. Lee. London: Penguin, 1965.

Plumb, J. H. *The Growth of Political Stability in England 1675–1725.* London: The History Book Club, 1968.

Primavesi, Anne. *Cultivating Unity within the Biodiversity of God.* Salem, OR: Polebridge, 2011.

———. *From Apocalypse to Genesis.* Tunbridge Wells: Burns & Oates, 1991.

———. *Gaia's Gift: Earth, Ourselves and God after Copernicus.* London: Routledge, 2003.

———. *Sacred Gaia: Holistic Theology and Earth System Science.* London: Routledge, 2000.

Rajotte, Freda. *First Nations Faith and Ecology.* London: Cassell, 1998.

Rawls, John. *Lectures on the History of Political Philosophy.* Cambridge, MA: Belknap, 2007.

Rockström, J., W. Steffen, K. Noone, Å. Persson, F. S. Chapin III, E. Lambin, T. M. Lenton, M. Scheffer, C. Folke, H. Schellnhuber, B. Nykvist, C. A. De Wit, T. Hughes, S. van der Leeuw, H. Rodhe, S. Sörlin, P. K. Snyder, R. Costanza, U. Svedin, M. Falkenmark, L. Karlberg, R. W. Corell, V. J. Fabry, J. Hansen, B. Walker, D. Liverman, K. Richardson, P. Crutzen, and J. Foley. "Planetary Boundaries: Exploring the Safe Operating Space for Humanity." No pages. Online: http://www.ecologyandsociety.org/vol14/iss2/art32/.

Ryan-Collins, Josh. *Where Does Money Come From?* London: New Economics Foundation, 2011.

Sandel, Michael J. *What Money Can't Buy: The Moral Limits of Markets.* London: Lane, 2012.

Scholder, Klaus. *The Churches and the Third Reich.* Translated by John Bowden. 2 vols. Vol. 1. London: SCM, 1987.

———. *A Requiem for Hitler and Other New Perspectives on the German Church Struggle.* London: SCM, 1989.

Schweitzer, Don. "Jonathan Edwards." In *Empire and the Christian Tradition: New Readings of Classical Theologians*, edited by Kwok Pui-lan, Don H. Compier, and Joerg Rieger, 243–55. Minneapolis: Fortress, 2007.

Suzuki, David, and Amanda McConnell. *The Sacred Balance: Rediscovering Our Place in Nature*. Vancouver: Greystone, 1997.

Thomas, Keith. *Man and the Natural World: Changing Attitudes in England 1500–1800*. Harmondsworth: Penguin, 1983.

Thurman, Howard. *Jesus and the Disinherited*. Boston: Beacon, 1976.

———. *Meditations of the Heart*. Boston: Beacon, 1981.

Valenze, Deborah. *The Social Life of Money in the English Past*. Cambridge: Cambridge University Press, 2006.

Walsham, Alexandra. *The Reformation of the Landscape: Religion, Identity and Memory in Early Modern Britain and Ireland*. Oxford: Oxford University Press, 2011.

Weber, Max. *The Protestant Ethic and the Spirit of Capitalism*. Translated by Talcott Parsons. London: Routledge, 1992.

Wink, Walter. "Facing the Myth of Redemptive Violence." No pages. Online: http://www.ekklesia.co.uk/content/cpt/article_060823wink.shtml.

Wordsworth, William. "Lines Composed a Few Miles above Tintern Abbey. July 13, 1798." No pages. Online: http://www.poetryfoundation.org/poem/174796.

Index